REBUILD
A 12-Part Framework for Rejuvenating and Restoring the Burnt-Out Pastor

MARCUS A. CYLAR, DMin

Copyright © 2015
Marcus A. Cylar

All rights reserved. No part of this book may be reproduced in any form without permission in writing from the publisher, except in the case of brief quotations embodied in critical articles or reviews.

All scripture quotations contained herein are from the New Revised Standard Version Bible, copyright © 1989, Division of Christian Education of the National Council of Churches of Christ in the U.S.A. Used by permission. All rights reserved.

All websites listed herein are accurate at the time of publication but may change in the future or cease to exist. The listing of website references and resources does not imply publisher endorsement of the site's entire contents. Groups and organizations are listed for informational purposes, and listing does not imply publisher endorsement of their activities.

ISBN-13: 978-0692414965

To the ladies of my life, for whom I do everything:
Chariece
Candace
Jada

&
Mom
[I'd do anything to be able to deliver this to you personally, but if there are books where you are, I'll leave one for you at the front gate. I hope you enjoy it.]

CONTENTS

Introduction — i

I Rebuild Your Psyche — 1

1. Timing — 3
   Am I really doing this?

2. Blame — 17
   Was it my fault?

3. Shame — 31
   How do I show my face again?

II Rebuild Your Foundation — 43

4. Family — 45
   Your first ministry

5. Community — 61
   Because we all need each other

6. Balance — 71
   More than just your position

III Rebuild Your Faith — 85

7. Rediscovery — 87
   Back to basics

8. Lessons — 99
   What would you do differently?

9. Ownership — 111
   Getting over it

IV Rebuild Your Life — 123

10. Story — 125
    How will you be defined?

11. Reinvention — 139
    God is not through with you yet

12. Reengagement — 157
    It's time to begin again

Notes — 169

Acknowledgments — 173

About the Author — 175

INTRODUCTION

I had taken over my most recent pastoral charge in Flint, Michigan in September 2012 after four successful years as a pastor, innovator, and district administrator in Canada. During my last year in Canada, I had ascended the administrative ranks to the office of Presiding Elder for the Canadian Conference of the 4th Episcopal District of the African Methodist Episcopal Church. At 29, I was by far the youngest in the denomination to serve in this capacity.

In every way except positionally, this move to Flint was widely considered an upgrade, and it was, as not only did my salary increase, but my struggles did, as well.

My ministry hell

By Thanksgiving, I was already in the throws of depression, having endured only a few brief but stressful, strife-filled months attempting to lead a people who largely rejected me because I was 30 years old, rather than 60+, the typical age of an acceptable pastor at this particular church. The next youngest pastor in the church's history was in his 40s, and like me, lasted only one year.

Earlier that month, I sat through two board meetings where 90 percent of my officers badmouthed me, criticized my every action in the previous two months of my pastorate, and called me just about everything but a child of God. From day one of my arrival at that church, a strong contingent of the congregation made it up in their minds that they were going to do everything possible to undermine my ministry and get me removed from there. My officers—the recognized lay leadership of the church—led the charge.

And to make matters worse, secret meetings were being held between members of the church and people in authority over me, discussing how they could remove me from the church. When I tried to expose this dishonest, undermining, backstabbing behavior to someone who had the power to do something about it, he blew it off without a second thought. He gave me a really weak reason why he found nothing wrong with the meetings, but by that point, he might as well had been speaking Swahili because I had stopped listening.

The previous year, I was trusted to serve in the position of Presiding Elder over a group of churches spread over three Canadian provinces, overseeing the conference's spiritual and financial affairs and leading the people through a few serious crises. I was trusted with the responsibility of being the youngest Presiding Elder in the denomination, yet when, yet in the face of obvious, well-documented corruption against me, I was not given anything closely resembling a vote of confidence.

It didn't matter that the youth and young adults, who had been disinterested for years, were coming alive and stepping up to positions of leadership.

It didn't matter that I was as trained (in all areas) and experienced (in most areas) as any pastor who had ever served there.

It didn't matter that my preaching, by the grace of God alone, was truly making a difference in the hearts and minds of those truly willing to listen.

The only thing that mattered to much of the membership was that I was young enough to be their grandson, so therefore, I couldn't possibly lead with any kind of authority.

By the beginning of June 2013, a few short days before the start of an under-supported, poorly attended Men's Day revival that many purposely decided to stay home from because I had planned it, I had fully realized that my tenure at this church would last no longer than one painfully short year.

It was at this point that I also began reading Michael Hyatt's blog and listening to his weekly podcast, "This is Your Life" [1]. I was so greatly edified by Hyatt's ability to weave his faith, experience, and innovation into his podcast that I found other similar podcasts and started listening to them all day, every day, on my hour-long commute to and from the church and while I worked in my office. It was only by God's grace that listening to hours and hours of podcasts every day kept me from throwing in the towel and giving up on ministry altogether.

My final three months pastoring this church were three of the hardest months of my life. I wanted to resign every day. Trying to stay motivated to do ministry at a place where I wasn't wanted was beyond difficult, but by the grace of God and the introduction of podcasts into my life, I made it through August 2013, the end of this most arduous conference year. Some days were harder than others, driving to and from the office with tears in my eyes, shortness of breath, and splitting headaches, but God was with me every step of the way.

Moving forward

One of the few things I had to hang on to during this season was the fact that I was in the middle of a Doctor of Ministry program, which, by the unmerited grace of God, I was able to complete while doing my research on issues related to pastoral burnout. I'm taking all I've been through and learned in this process and distilling it into several publications, the first of which is this book. I am by no means the foremost expert in pastoral burnout or in counseling those who have endured burnout—I'm still going through the process myself—but God has given me a perspective, a 12-part framework for overcoming burnout that has helped me tremendously and that I pray will help many others.

Book roadmap

Rebuild comprises 12 chapters, 12 different aspects of the life of a burnt-out pastor that need attention during the burnout experience. These chapters are grouped into four sections containing three chapters each; the sections, each of which will be explained in greater detail, are specific areas that need to be rebuilt.

This book is equal parts autobiography, self-help guide,

devotional, and resource manual. To that effect, every chapter contains the following elements: biblical reference, theological reflection based mostly on that reference, practical application from personal experiences, and devotional points. The devotional points portion concludes each chapter and comprises the following: *reflect* – points to think about regarding the chapter, *read* – related scriptures and other resources, and *pray* – #PrayForYourPastor and personal prayer from me.

Obviously, the #PrayForYourPastor point needs a little explanation. If you follow that hashtag anywhere on social media, you'll find a number of graphics with statistics highlighting burnout in pastoral ministry and the various prevalent issues that cause it. This short section of every chapter is specifically for any laypeople who may read this book and have a desire and opportunity to help their pastor. As each of these topics is related to burnout and burnout recovery, each also presents opportunities for laypeople in the local church to take particular actions or make certain mindset shifts to help their pastors maintain peace, stay motivated, and be less inclined to burn out.

The primary audience for this book is pastors who have suffered burnout in their ministries, resigned from their positions, and need a guide to help them as they strive to regain some semblance of an identity and normal life after such a traumatic experience. But while I do have a specific audience I'm looking to reach with this book, my prayer is that (a) pastors currently still in their positions find the book useful for helping them avoid burnout, and that (b) current pastors on the verge of burning out will read this book, learn from my story, and reverse course on several areas so they can avoid burnout.

I also want laypeople to read this book so they can understand just how integral they and their fellow church members are to the health of the ministry and the sanity of their pastor. When lay members are strong, faithful, prayerful, and helpful, rather than conniving, divisive, mean-spirited, and sabotaging, they help create an environment whereby the pastor is fully able to do the work of ministry. And when a pastor has members who are neither adversaries nor yes men and yes women, but who work honestly with the man or woman of God to effectively build the kingdom and help the ministry grow, he or she is far less likely to experience burnout. I offer points of consideration for laypeople to help in this endeavor.

What this book is not

This book is by no means the definitive guide on burnout in pastoral ministry, nor do I even pretend to masquerade as the preeminent authority on the subject. What I am, though, is someone who has endured burnout in a very real way and whose ministerial career deteriorated into shambles because of local church conflict and lack of support from key people who could have intervened.

I didn't write *Rebuild* to distill decades of knowledge on the subject of burnout; I wrote it to tell my story and to share with the world the framework for recovery that God has downloaded into my spirit on my road to rebuilding my life and ministry from complete ruin to a place of vitality and productivity. I pray this labor of love blesses you, resonates with your own experience, and compels you to pass on the message that there is abundant life after burnout.

MARCUS A. CYLAR, DMIN
DETROIT, MICHIGAN
MARCH 2015

Introduction

I
REBUILD YOUR PSYCHE

Burnout leading to resignation from pastoral ministry is a traumatic experience, and when it happens, the pastor undoubtedly goes through the gamut of emotions, some of the stronger ones most likely being anger at the members of the church from which he or she resigned, disillusionment with God and/or the institutional church altogether, and fear about the future, not knowing what he or she is going to do to make a living moving forward.

Before the man or woman of God can even begin to heal, steps must be taken to rebuild the psyche, to get his or her mental faculties in order to be able to deal with the rest of the steps in the rebuilding process.

CYLAR

-1-
TIMING
Am I really doing this?
"Then Joshua tore his clothes, and fell to the ground on his face before the ark of the Lord until the evening, he and the elders of Israel; and they put dust on their heads."
Joshua 7:6

THEOLOGICAL REFLECTION

Joshua is certainly not the first biblical leader you think of when considering the subject of pastoral burnout. Joshua was a very successful leader whose faithfulness was honored by God, as God favored him, along with Caleb, to be the only men of their generation to survive the entire 40-year wilderness journey from Egypt to the Promised Land.

He translated his faithfulness into powerful, effective leadership, as he took the mantle from Moses and led the Israelites into the Promised Land of Canaan, wherein he had to engage in numerous battles to defeat the occupants of that land God had given them before they could possess it. In every battle, at every turn, Joshua and the people of Israel were successful.

Except this one time.

Joshua had just defeated the inhabitants of the city of Jericho with strength, shrewd strategy, and the help of the

Lord. This was the very first battle for Joshua and the Israelites after crossing over into the land, and they knew it was going to be a difficult battle, but they did what they had to do for a victorious first conquest.

As challenging as that battle was, the next one in the city of Ai ought to have been a piece of cake, and Joshua surmised as such when the men he sent out gave him the report about the lay of the Land. The city was small and the inhabitants few, so Joshua, trying to use his resources efficiently, deployed only a few thousand men, a relative handful of Israelites.

The battle at Ai was anything but easy, however, as 36 Israelites were killed in battle. Joshua just knew this should not have happened, and it really discouraged him. Verses 6-7 of chapter seven say he tore his clothes, fell on his face, and cried out to God. God promised to be with Joshua every step of the way, so why would God seemingly leave him in such an easy battle, so soon in the journey of conquering the land of Canaan? So thought Joshua.

After Joshua cried out, God let him know exactly what the problem was—there was sin in the camp because one of the men had blatantly disobeyed God—and told him exactly what he needed to do to handle the situation. The next day, Joshua, as we see repeatedly throughout the chronicles of his leadership, followed God's commands to the letter, identified and eliminated the culprit, and got his people and himself back in right standing with God. Every battle thereafter, big or small, was successful.

Theologically, this is not an illustration of burnout in pastoral ministry. Joshua was not a leader experiencing burnout in any way; he had simply run into a surprisingly challenging situation that discouraged him a little bit because of how easy it should have been and how soon it came in the journey. Leaders are always cautioned to keep their feet firmly planted on the ground and not allow every little adverse situation sway them back and forth and question their calling or relationship with God. But that's not the issue here. Joshua knew that.

The important point to extract from this illustration for this context is that Joshua had sense enough to lean not to his own understanding and take his vulnerability straight to God. When we face challenging circumstances, we have a tendency to insert our own inadequate strength and wisdom into what we're going through, rather than taking our problems to God and letting God either handle them outright or give us the tools and the insight to find resolution.

That battle at Ai was one measly little battle wherein Joshua lost a mere 36 men out of 3,000. He could have just tried another tactic or simply sent more men the next day, but he had the wisdom to understand those 36 casualties had nothing to do with a tactical error or manpower deficiency, but were symbolic of a deeper spiritual issue that needed to be handled with prayer and reflection before more lives were lost.

Joshua's timing couldn't have been better. He dealt with the root of his problem early on in his journey and avoided potential catastrophe.

When you're on the cusp of burnout, of course, you find yourself in a situation far worse than what Joshua faced. You're likely in constant conflict with the people you're leading, you might be facing equal or greater conflict at home, you're overworked and your physical health is probably not where it should be, and you're discouraged about ministry and possibly about life in general.

Simply put, if you're on the decline to burnout, you're in no mental or spiritual state to be trying to solve problems on your own and put your own wisdom into your current situation. Now is the time to retreat, tear your clothes (if you have to), fall on your face, and cry out to God. You may feel you've done so much wrong and that it's too late to call on the Lord, but it's never too late to talk to God.

The first step in the rebuilding process from burnout is to consider timing. Resigning from a church is a major decision, so before making it, get in the face of God and storm heaven in fervent prayer. Assess whether or not you're really facing burnout, and if you are, take some considerable time to figure out (a) what needs to happen right now and in the future for you to stay and (b) how to exit gracefully if you know you need to leave.

Not every burnout situation requires an exit from pastoral ministry. You may just need to take a brief sabbatical to take inventory of your life and ministry and make necessary changes for you to continue in a healthy way that will secure your longevity. You may need to swallow your pride, sit some people down, and have some tough conversations with them in attempts to repair some breaches. It may be too late. The breaches may be beyond repair. But God will let you know that in prayer.

Do this before it's too late. Timing is everything.

PRACTICAL APPLICATION

Future Hall-of-Fame quarterback Brett Favre enjoyed a legendary career, winning a Super Bowl and setting numerous passing records with the Green Bay Packers. The "Gunslinger" was famous for taking chances on the football field, wiggling out of some tight spots and throwing into even tighter ones.

Toward the end of his career, however, he struggled mightily with the decision to retire or continue playing, putting his team and football fans across America on an annual Brett Favre "retirement watch". For several consecutive offseasons, General Manager Ted Thompson was forced to wonder whether his star signal caller would be hanging up his cleats or would suit up for another campaign at a second Super Bowl ring before riding off into the sunset.

Often, this wondering, this ambiguity, this cloud of confusion lingering over the organization lasted until training camp, when he would suddenly decide to play again and waltz in to the team facilities after leaving everyone in limbo all summer long. One offseason unfolded just a little bit differently, though, as Favre finally announced his retirement following the season.

But Thompson was prepared for this announcement because a few years prior, knowing the end was near for the face of the franchise, he astutely used the team's first-round draft pick on Aaron Rodgers, an immensely talented but largely unheralded prospect out of the University of California. What the GM was not prepared for, though, was for Favre to change his mind and declare he was coming back.

Thompson called Favre's bluff and kindly let the legend know that if he was going to come out of his two-month retirement, he would do so as the backup to Rodgers, who had been training all summer long as the presumed starting quarterback for the Packers. Thompson made the courageous but wise decision that it was time to move on from Brett Favre.

As great as Favre had been for the Packers over his entire career, Thompson understood that if the franchise was going to remain competitive long term, he could not allow the 3-time MVP to hold them hostage and stunt the development of Aaron Rodgers, his successor.

After being informed he'd be unable to simply slide back into his starting position, Favre stormed into Thompson's office and shouted, "Do you know who I am?"

Well, that might not actually have been said, but one could imagine a conversation between them going such a way. Thompson called Favre's bluff, and after a long battle, Favre found himself with the New York Jets for one potentially promising but ultimately underwhelming season. Many thought the Gunslinger would retire after a disappointing end to that season, but he was determined to keep playing and keep chasing that elusive second ring.

The Minnesota Vikings won the rights to his services for two seasons, the first of which was arguably the best of his career, and the second, his 20th and final season, a poor showing cut woefully short by injury. Many argue he shouldn't even have played that last season because during the previous year, he barely missed returning to the Super Bowl, and at his advanced age, it was very unlikely he'd be able to replicate the individual and team accomplishments of that season. A simple perusal of his career statistics bare that fact out.

Brett Favre will go down as one of the greatest quarterbacks of all time. The way he left the game, however—kicking and screaming—left a bad taste in many fans' mouths, especially those who revered him in Green Bay. Favre didn't know when to say when, and because of that, he tarnished his legacy, maybe not in the long term, but certainly in the short term.

~ ~ ~

Any time I think about timing relative to my own experiences, Favre is such an easy example for me. As an ordinary football fan, it was very easy to see some of the negative effects hanging on too long had on Favre.

I did not want that for myself. Especially when people's souls were on the line.

My final year of pastoral ministry was at a place where I was set up to fail, not by everyone there—I had some major allies I still consider family today—but certainly by those who had the influence, the money, and the power to make things happen. Although it was rumored that I didn't want to be there, I was truly excited to be at this church because I could look around and see that everyone and everything we needed to fulfill the vision was already there.

It was all a matter of preaching the unadulterated, uncompromising word of God to them on a regular basis, sparking a change in their hearts, making the vision plain to them, recognizing the people's spiritual gifts, and mobilizing them to action based on those gifts. That's the change I was attempting to lead at the church. Unfortunately, I was never given the chance to do so.

And twelve mere months a chance does not make.

I should've known…

I really cared about the people, and I wanted to make things work, but that wasn't God's ultimate plan for me at this charge. Now that I've had the past year and a half to reflect over all I've been through, I can look back and see a number of clear signs that it just wasn't going to happen.

When I learned that several of my members had regular communication with my superior, whether or not they ever came to my office, I should've known things weren't looking good.

When I had to endure the ministry equivalent of a trip to the principal's office to discuss a number of petty issues brought to my superior's attention by obstructive members, only to meet with my stewards ten days later over those same issues, I should've known things weren't looking good.

When I received a wonderful 4-page letter of support in the mail from an officer telling me this individual felt compelled to send a copy of the letter to my top superior, I should've known things weren't looking good (because all the other letters that had been sent to his office were negative).

When I pulled into the church parking lot in January of the following calendar year, a full four months after my appointment to the church, and could see that the marquee had not been changed to reflect that I was the pastor, I should have known things weren't looking good. (I never really cared about things like that, but looking back on everything, it was certainly a factor.)

When I received a call from an officer talking asking me if I knew about a meeting between other officers and my superior—at another church on the other side of the city, mind you—that I had not been informed about, I *knew* things weren't looking good.

When my wife told me the owner of a store she and a member were shopping at one day said the following to her: "Are you the new First Lady over at [XYZ] Church? I heard things haven't been going well over there," I knew things weren't looking good.

When a member came to my office one day to let me know how disappointed this individual was that people this person was talking to while on vacation in a completely different state, nowhere near the state of Michigan were discussing rumors they had heard about me, once again, I knew things weren't looking good.

In other words, the assault against my ministry had gone nationwide.

Not a minute longer

So, when the final quarter of the year came and things had not gotten any better, nor were there any signs that things could get better, I knew my days were numbered.

I had a few very supportive ministry colleagues who knew what I was going through, who understood my pain, and tried to speak some words of encouragement to me to hang in there and keep going.

One colleague in particular had this to say:

"Hang in there, young man. I know it's hard right now, but I'm believing God that Bishop will send you back for year two. And when he does, you'll be able to have more influence over your officers. You'll be able to put the people you want in certain spots and make some things happen."

This colleague meant well. All my supportive colleagues meant well. They were seasoned veterans in pastoral ministry and knew how to navigate the ebbs and flows that come with the vocation.

But this wasn't about influence. This wasn't about positioning and mobilizing "my" people. This wasn't about hoping and praying and waiting on pins and needles for a Bishop to make a decision about my future long after influential intervention could have taken place.

This was about my life and the lives of those under my spiritual care.

Let's start with the latter. The people who supported my ministry and had absolutely nothing to do with the conflict that was tearing the church apart didn't deserve to be stuck in an atmosphere wherein they could not grow in Christ because of the constant barrage of negativity.

With me, I just couldn't take another year of the conflict. My health was fading, my wife and I were at each other's throats every night, I had no peace, and I was depressed.

As clear as I'm making the decision sound in this reflection, it certainly wasn't so. I agonized over the decision to resign. I didn't want to let people down, I didn't want to look like a quitter, I didn't want to communicate to my colleagues and to the body of Christ that I did not trust God, and, quite frankly, I didn't want to lose a steady paycheck. I have a young family.

With each passing day, it became clearer and clearer leaving was the right thing to do. Had I had just one inkling of hope that things would get better, had I gotten a vote of confidence from those in authority over me, I just might have been able to stick it out. After all, I'm surely not the first to have dealt with major church conflict from people resistant to progress. In fact, Thom Rainer's *Breakout Churches* is full of examples of churches who were able to ride the waves of conflict, division, and temporary loss of membership, only to come out bigger, stronger, better on the other side.

It could be done, but it wasn't going to happen for me. So, when I finally learned that the plan was indeed to transfer me to a different church for the next conference year, I decided to take a break from the itinerancy altogether. Who was to say the next church wouldn't do the same thing and that I would receive the same lack of institutional support? I couldn't put my family through that again. I couldn't put myself through that again.

I left at the absolute right time. Trying to beg and plead for another year to try to make things right would have just meant more heartache, more angst, more pain for everyone. And for what? Just to prove I could do it? Just to show everyone I wasn't a quitter? No, not with people's souls on the line.

I'll admit, the analogy between Brett Favre and me

crumbles on one key point. Favre enjoyed a Hall-of-Fame career, but just didn't know when or how to walk away from the game he so deeply loved. I, on the other hand, made a decision that added me to the ranks of the 1,500 pastors who leave vocational ministry every single month. Certainly nothing extraordinary about that.

Where the analogy holds water, though, is in the timing aspect of decision making. Because Favre didn't know when to retire, he damaged the relationship, at least temporarily, with the franchise he led valiantly for so many years, and added more and more wear and tear to his body, ultimately causing it to make the decision to retire for him.

Because I knew when to walk away, I did not allow my deep depression to bleed all over the members of that church or of the subsequent church to which I would have been sent. I allowed those who tirelessly supported me to remember my family and me as beacons of hope, as positive change agents, as people who cared about them, as friends. I regained sanity and vitality. By walking away at the right time, I just might have saved my marriage.

Every day of the week, I'll take being the guy who left the party too early over being the one who overstayed his welcome. Let us never let the anticipation of pain preclude us from making the decisions that absolutely must be made. Learn from my pain.

DEVOTIONAL POINTS

Reflect

1. Think about all you've done in pastoral ministry. Think about the good and bad times. Do the bad times truly outweigh the good, or is it really vice versa? If it's the former, will identifying and solving the root problem that led to the bad times help you to recover from the burnout? In other words, is the situation at your church beyond repair with you at the helm or not?

2. When have you ever quit something too late or too soon? What happened as a result?

3. Compare the times you took a problem straight to God and let God handle it to when you inserted your own wisdom into the situation and tried to solve it yourself. Will doing the former at this point in your ministry help you stay, or do you know it's truly time to go?

Read
1. Joshua 6-8.
2. Blog post, "9 Signs You're Burning Out in Leadership," by Carey Nieuwhof. This leading pastor, blogger, and podcaster wrote this first of two posts based on his own experience of burnout in ministry. He wrote the post back in 2013, but it still gets regular hits, social media shares, and comments because it's a very candid and informative article. It's *the* article you need to read before making a decision.
3. PastorBurnout.com. If you search "pastor burnout" in your search engine of choice, this website will come up first. It's a fantastic site with statistics, facts, tips, and resources related to burnout in pastoral ministry. One of the best features on the site, though, is a section of anonymously submitted burnout stories that candidly cover just about every scenario you could think of regarding people who are at their wits' end in ministry. The stories can be quite discouraging, but it's good to read them to get a good idea of just where you are and how much more you can really handle.

Pray
#PrayForYourPastor
Pray fervently for your pastor. Whatever your relationship is with your pastor or however you feel about him or her, you should pray that he or she hears from God clearer than ever before and makes the right decision for him/her and his/her family. Pray for God to help you make your pastor's exit as smooth and amicable as possible if he or she decides to leave, or to help you make your pastor's experience better if he or she decides to stay. More than likely, your pastor wants to do

a good job, wants to bring souls to Christ, wants to grow the church, cares about you, cares about your soul. What can you do to help him or her make that happen without burning out?

My prayer for you...

Father, in the name of Jesus, I thank you for life, I thank you for health, and I thank you for strength. I thank you for everything you allowed me to go through and for strengthening me to endure it. I thank you for the opportunity to recover to the point where I can now share this material with those who are now in the same position I was once in.

My prayer for your pastors on the verge of burnout is that you would, first of all, wrap them up in your arms like never before. Reassure them that you have not left and are still there for hem. Give them the clarity of mind and spirit to make the right decision to either stay and make changes or walk away peacefully and make those changes in private.

Should it be your will for your servants to stay and not retreat, help them with the power of your Holy Spirit to endure whatever conflict they face presently, and endow them with the strength and courage to make the challenging decisions and have the difficult conversations necessary for substantive change to take place. Favor these leaders among the people they serve and warm their hearts toward their pastor so that change and healing can take place. Regardless of what has happened in the past, unite pastor and people under your vision for them and help them communicate clearly and honestly with one another so the church can move forward.

If any of these pastors absolutely need to leave, give them the courage to make that decision, even though that could mean leaving money on the table. Shift circumstances to allow them to be able to exit in a way that is neither embarrassing, nasty, vengeful, nor hurtful for them or the church. Have your way in this most important decision, and help your servants to deal with consequences thereof as gracefully as possible. I ask all these things in Jesus' name, Amen.

Timing

-2-
BLAME

Was it my fault?
"Then Job answered:
'How long will you torment me,
and break me in pieces with words?
These ten times you have cast reproach upon me;
are you not ashamed to wrong me?
And even if it is true that I have erred,
my error remains with me.
If indeed you magnify yourselves against me,
and make my humiliation an argument against me,
know then that God has put me in the wrong,
and closed his net around me.'"
Job 19:1-6

THEOLOGICAL REFLECTION

The 30,000-foot view of the point of the book of Job is that it's a story of a man who loses everything but never turned his back on God. Job is an honorable man, living a good life of integrity and high character, only to be tested in losing his children and all his material possessions. Job remains faithful, however, and after his season of trial received double of all he had lost.

The story goes much deeper than that, though. There are

definitely some instances when Job doesn't have the best attitude toward his situation or toward God, and God holds Job accountable for that attitude with a long lecture toward the end of the narrative. Job's internal conflict about what he was going through is certainly understandable and probably not much different than how any of us would have acted had we endured a similar season of loss.

Perhaps you've already been through such a season and actually did curse the day you were born, just like Job, so you understand even more how Job was feeling. God understands, too, which is why God ultimately blesses him.

What's most important about this scripture and most relevant to the discussion of pastoral burnout is how terribly Job's friends fail him when he needs them most. Job's friends first appear in the narrative in 2:11-13, and they come off favorably, sitting with Job seven days and seven nights without saying a word. True friends know how to just sit with you sometimes and let you go through your emotions to process what's going on, knowing there's not much you can say when someone has just lost everything. The ministry of presence is a powerful one.

This ministry doesn't last very long, though, for after those seven days, when Job's friends see that Job is still in a fragile emotional state and begins to speak negatively in that fragility, their support wanes, and they begin criticizing Job for his poor mindset and blaming him for all that's happened to him.

Job's friends perhaps make some solid points about how Job shouldn't have questioned God and that his attitude in general should have been better, but theologically, that criticism is mildly important, at best. One of the major takeaways from the book of Job is that regardless of how right his friends might be, they fail Job because at his weakest moment, what he needed from them most was their support, not their pseudo-righteousness.

And God lets Job's friends know this when God commands the men to submit a burnt offering unto God, for which Job would pray. The men wanted Job to humble himself before God, but ultimately the friends were the ones required to humble themselves before God and before Job.

When you experience the pain of burnout in and exit from pastoral ministry, one of the first emotions you deal with is that of blame. You blame certain people for not supporting you, but even more so, you blame yourself because it's a really easy thing to do. When you become a pastor, you think you'll be doing that for the rest of your life or until retirement, so when you resign from the pastorate, you blame yourself because you feel like you've let God and yourself down.

And it can be even harder to deal with this feeling of blame if you don't have the kind of support system that will truly hold you up when you're weakest. Job certainly didn't have that kind of group, as Job's friends and even his wife were extremely critical of him in a season when he just needed their love.

At this point in the process of rebuilding from burnout, what you need more than anything is love and support. You have plenty of time for introspection, repentance, and self-improvement, but right now, you need love, and you need to stop blaming yourself because while you're in a state of condemnation, your mind and spirit are not open to learning what you need to in order to go to the next level in the rebuilding process. God wasn't able to really speak to Job in the latter chapters of the book until he stopped the self-loathing talk from some of the earlier chapters.

As Job illustrated, when you descend to your lowest, darkest moments, the people you've always counted on just might not be there for you, and you may have no one to lift you up but God. Let God do the work of encouraging you and don't succumb to the negativity. You just focus on not losing your mind in this most difficult season and not allowing blame, either from others or from yourself, keep you processing all you've been through and learning what you need to learn from it.

PRACTICAL APPLICATION

Have you ever dated someone long enough to where you had the opportunity to introduce that person to your friends and family, yet you didn't quite make it down the aisle with him or her?

If you've been in that situation before, but you're married now, then more than likely, you've introduced multiple significant others to your loved ones. With more than one "special someone" to meet, you've given your friends and family an opportunity for comparison, whether intentionally or unintentionally.

There are two ways the instance of comparison can go, and both of them are equally funny, if you ask me.

Scenario A:
Friend: Hey, how's it going with Tracey?
You: I'm not with Tracey anymore. I'm with Stacey now.
Friend: Oh, okay, cool, man. I didn't really like Tracey that much anyway.
You: Really? I thought you said she was cool…

Scenario B:
Friend 1: Yeah, I really enjoyed meeting your girl the other day.
You: Stacey?
Friend 1: Yeah, Stacey. She was really nice. I like her much better than who you were with before.
Friend 2: Oh yeah, the new girl is way better than the old girl!
You: <shrugs and chuckles>

There's nothing that brings out negative comments quite like transitioning from old to new. As long as you are in any way affiliated with someone, be it through an organization, fellowship, fraternity, or group of any kind, one will more than likely refrain from making negative comments about the other.

If you're on a team with someone you don't like, or if someone you care for is in a relationship with an individual you don't care very much for, you're probably going to keep your feelings to yourself, unless you're one of the few who never has a problem telling people what you think, even if you know it will anger them.

But when the person in question is no longer on your team anymore? Oh yeah, all bets are off.

We see it all the time with failed marriages, corporate splits and/or CEO firings, front-office or player personnel moves on sports teams, and defeats in political elections. We also observe this in a most ugly fashion with respect to the hiring and firing or transfer of pastors.

When you are forced into some form of affiliation with a person for whom you don't have a high regard, and you're both a part of a larger team or organization, you know it's typically in the best interest of the group to keep your personal feelings about that individual to yourself. Despite how you feel about someone on your team, especially someone in leadership, you care about the success of that team, and you're willing to suppress your personal feelings for a season if getting along is what's best for the team at the time.

So the moment you're no longer affiliated with that individual and your obligations to him or her have therefore ended, you experience the sweetest relief. You can finally let go of the inflated balloon of emotions you've been holding in with the mere pinch of your thumb and index finger for days, months, or even years. Thank God, you can let that air out!

The newfound opportunity this change has afforded you to speak your mind, to verbalize the unflattering things you have to say about that one person you just can't stand has given you a jolt of energy rivaling the shot the strongest cup of Starbucks coffee delivers to a tired morning commuter's nervous system.

After the personnel change has been made, after the trade has gone down, after the embattled pastor has been let go or transferred to another church, you just can't wait until the next meeting or next opportunity to come together because you just have to tell everybody what's been on your mind that you just couldn't say before.

I know for sure that's how a number of people felt when I resigned.

I know there were at least four individuals—a group of people who otherwise would not have attended the annual conference, but who just had to go to this one in particular to petition the Bishop to get rid of me—who breathed the biggest sigh of relief when the announcement about my resignation was made on the conference floor.

I can imagine they gave each other hugs and high-fives, patted each other on the back, congratulated one another on a job well done, laughed and sang songs on their 90-minute commute back home, and enjoyed a satisfying dinner with their families that evening. They were overjoyed, relieved, and probably surprised they didn't have to spend the entire weekend back and forth to the conference to stay in the Bishop's face to beg desperately for a change.

They did it. They got me out of there. They got their church back.

You see, this is the story I've played out in my mind over and over again. God has blessed me with a keen self-awareness to know exactly what my faults and shortcomings are as a person. If you ask my wife, she'll probably tell you my self-awareness is to a fault. I don't accentuate the positive nearly enough and dwell way too much on the negative.

In this case, though, I felt I had to be self-aware because, even as a pastor in conflict, I had very few detractors who actually had the courage to make an appointment, come to my office, sit down, look me in my face, and tell me what they thought of me. The people who were most in disagreement with my ministry, with how I conducted my business, with how I preached, with how I prioritized family life, with me in general, either never came to church, or never talked to me one-on-one.

My detractors were more content talking about me to keep up conflict than they were talking to me to end conflict.

So, I've absolutely had to be self-aware. I've had to look myself in the mirror, look deep within myself, and figure out why I couldn't get enough people to buy into the vision. I had to figure out if there was anything else about me besides my age that made me such a pariah at this church that I couldn't last longer than one short year.

One person in particular had the courage to speak from the heart. These comments have stuck with me to this day:

> *"Rev. Cylar, the fact of the matter is you didn't get off to a quick start when you first arrived here. Whatever reasons you had, or whatever you had going on in your personal life at the time, you weren't ready to go to work. You didn't come out of the gate very strong at all. You have to deal with that."*

I've had countless moments of introspection, many nights of prayer about those words. They came in the form of a strongly worded email I foolishly opened right before I sat down with my family one afternoon to eat at BD's Mongolian Barbecue. I shouldn't have even looked at my phone.

My dinner was ruined.

While I was very disappointed to be looking at this unbelievably blunt email, I really had to pause, step back, and take a look at myself. Was I really ready to pastor this church? Did I give it my all? Did I put too many things above my ministry responsibilities? Did I take ministry seriously?

The more I look back at how everything unfolded, the more I consider all that I said and that was said to me, the more I ask these questions, the stronger my initial conclusion becomes. I was in a unique, possibly unprecedented situation that I assert few at my station in life could handle.

Imagine...

Imagine sitting quietly in your home office, studying and preparing the following Sunday's sermon, when your Bishop calls you completely out of the blue and informs you, a 29-year-old, third-year pastor, five months into parenthood, that he needs you to step in as Acting Presiding Elder for your Annual Conference that's coming up in less than three weeks.

Imagine putting your life on hold, jumping on your phone, diving into your email, burning the midnight oil, and doing all the leg work necessary to ensure a successful conference under your watch. Imagine executing well enough on this that your Bishop goes ahead, removes the interim tag, and elevates you to the full office of Presiding Elder. At 29 years old.

Imagine having well-laid, innovative plans for the office, but by the same token, having very much to fly by the seat of your pants with no orientation and little training because your predecessor is busy literally fighting for his life and, shortly thereafter, mourning the sudden, tragic loss of his youngest son.

Imagine stumbling, learning, growing, leading, all while finding out your wife is getting ready to have your second baby girl in less than two years, and helping her through an absolutely debilitating pregnancy, all while traveling constantly back and forth between international borders to meetings, conferences, and seminars, at home and abroad.

Imagine finding out at the end of the conference year that you're getting ready to be moved. You don't know exactly when or where, but you know it's coming.

Imagine preparing for one of your best friends' wedding and wanting desperately to be there for him and fulfill your commitment to him as a groomsman, despite all that's happening.

Imagine knowing for certain your wife is not going to carry your unborn baby a full 40 weeks, but praying she holds on long enough so you can fulfill all of your responsibilities and still witness the birth of your baby girl.

Imagine all of this transition happening at one time, all of these life events converging into the span of just a few short days:

- Finding out the church to which you're being moved Saturday

- Saying goodbye to your old church and receiving the appointment for your new church Sunday
- Attempting to schedule a Meet and Greet with your new church but not being able to because your wife is admitted to the hospital after her doctor's appointment Monday
- Welcoming your new baby girl to the world Tuesday evening
- Jumping on a plane across the country Thursday
- Standing up for the wedding Saturday
- Flying back in town Sunday (not in time for service, unfortunately, and probably to the chagrin of many)

I've never heard of a pastor welcoming a child into the world just two days after receiving an appointment. Most of my colleagues either answered their call to ministry well after having their children or were comfortably into their tenure at whatever church they were leading when their children were born.

I tried to stress to people over and over again that I was in an unusual situation and that I needed a little bit of a grace period while getting acclimated to a new church, a new city, a new child, a wife with new cuts from a second caesarean section birth in 17 months, and altogether new circumstances. The people who were supportive totally understood my situation, saw how hard I was working, even if they didn't see me physically in the office every day, and had no problem extending me that grace. Those looking to get rid of me weren't interested in any of that.

For my adversaries, if I didn't arrive at the office when they wanted me to as often as they wanted me there, if I didn't wear the right thing to church, if I didn't do what they wanted me to do when they wanted it done, I was going to hear about it, first from the Steward Board, then from my superiors.

Never once did any of these critical individuals ask how I was doing or if I needed any assistance with anything.

Pastor, how are you doing?

Pastor, can we help you with anything?

Pastor, how is your transition coming? Is there anything we can do to make that easier for you?

Pastor, how is your wife doing? Is there anything we can do for her?

Pastor, how's the new baby? Can we do something for her? Is there anything she needs?

Pastor, I know there's really no one at home to help your wife with the children while she recovers. Go on and take some time to be with your family and work from home.

Nope. None of that.

No benefit of the doubt

I need you to understand what I'm saying here. I'm not saying anyone was required to do anything for me. If that's what you're thinking, and you somehow believe I'm showing my millennial sense of entitlement, then I'm afraid I might not be able to reach you. What I'm saying is when you make an investment in someone, you commit yourself to navigating through challenges and through ups and downs with that person, believing things will altogether work out for good.

When you're looking to cut someone off at the knees and prove he or she doesn't belong, you'll find you'll never be short of opportunities to do so because it's very easy to identify the negative in every situation.

In the hearts and minds of many at this church, I was never going to be their pastor. I could have walked on water, and they still would have badmouthed me, disrespected my wife, ridiculed my children, and spread rumors about me all over the country.

In my tendency toward perfectionism, I always seek insight about my faults, my shortcomings, my contributions to whatever negative circumstance in which I may find myself. I don't think I've second-guessed myself more about anything in my life than I have about the 12 months I spent at this church. What I've taken away from all this second guessing is another story for another day.

The healing process from this ordeal has taken a very long time, but one of the realizations that has helped more than any is that in no uncertain terms, I was part of a setup, and there was nothing I was ever going to be able to do to win some people.

No longer blaming myself

I stopped blaming myself once I realized the senior tenured member of the church was never going to see me as anything other than a boy. I stopped blaming myself once I realized nothing I could have possibly done was going to prevent one officer from leaving the sanctuary and sitting downstairs while I preached. Or another officer from just not coming to church at all.

I stopped blaming myself for the tough decisions I did not make and for the people who criticized me for not making them because I know for certain I didn't have the backing of my leadership to do the things that needed to be done to make the church better.

In the book *Pastors in Transition: Why Clergy Leave Local Church Ministry*, Hoge and Wenger state, along with many other pastoral burnout statistics, that according to denominational officials, pastors who had left denominational ministry were largely loners in their fellowship and rarely a part of ministerial friendship groups.

That may be true, as loneliness and isolationism play huge roles in the burnout experience, but what I've gone through personally, beyond the statistics, makes me wonder if some of these denominational leaders use the "He/she was a loner anyway" statement to make themselves feel better about pastoral attrition and their potential role in it. Just something to think about.

I'm not pointing blame at anybody for what I've been through. The people who were responsible for various things in this situation already know what their roles were. What I'm no longer doing, either, is blaming myself.

DEVOTIONAL POINTS
Reflect
1. Think about—but don't dwell on—everything you went through in pastoral ministry for which you could indeed blame yourself. Once you've thought about it this one time, let it go. Stop blaming yourself. No one deserves to be in pain, and your pain will only get worse the more you blame yourself. Give it to God and let God begin to heal you.

2. What are the people closest to you saying? Are they tearing you down (whether knowingly or unknowingly) by criticizing your fragile (at this point) mindset and pointing out all the places where you fell short, or are they lifting you up through the ministry of presence or through positive reinforcement? They may mean well, but if your closest friends or those you keep in your circle are denigrating you more than they're elevating you, you need to let them go and pull back from them for the moment. This is too fragile a time for you to subject yourself to unwarranted, unnecessary criticism.

Read
1. The entire book of Job.
2. *Clergy Killers* by G. Lloyd Rediger. This book talks extensively about pastors who are sabotaged a small contingent of people in some churches who play the game of divide and conquer and deceptively thwart the pastor at every turn to prevent him or her from doing any real ministry in the church and keeping the entire congregation stuck in neutral. Being in such an environment was what led to my burnout and resignation from pastoral ministry. Perhaps this was not your root cause, but it was definitely mine. But if you identify, it might encourage you to know that other experienced, well-trained pastors have gone through just like you have and that your situation is not unique.

Pray
#PrayForYourPastor

Do you blame your pastor for everything wrong in your church, or do you know those who do? Any time your pastor makes a mistake, do you take it personally and criticize him or her for it, or do you charge it to his or her humanity and extend him or her grace? Pray for your pastor's strength constantly and pray that he or she will be empowered to make sound ministry decisions without fear of what everyone is going to think. Pray for the strength to do your part to create an atmosphere throughout the church that empowers your pastor to function without the weight of constant criticism. Pray for the courage to approach your pastor or make an appointment to talk honestly and openly to him or her when you have an issue instead of letting it fester or gossiping behind his or her back about the issue with people who have neither power nor authority to deal with it appropriately.

My prayer for you…

Father, in the name of the Lord Jesus Christ, strengthen these burnt out pastors. Your servants have made the decision to depart from pastoral ministry and may possibly be at the lowest point in their lives. Encourage your servants and remove the spirit of blame from above their heads. Remove, either temporarily or permanently, those with no sensitivity who would rather focus on the negative and blame your servant for everything that went wrong than encourage them in this most bleak season. Take away all blame from this pastor's heart and free up his or her mind to receive whatever insight you have for them. Let your children know you still love them and you're not through with them yet. This I pray in Jesus' name, Amen.

Blame

-3-
SHAME
How do I show my face again?

"When morning came, all the chief priests and the elders of the people conferred together against Jesus in order to bring about his death. They bound him, led him away, and handed him over to Pilate the governor. When Judas, his betrayer, saw that Jesus was condemned, he repented and brought back the thirty pieces of silver to the chief priests and the elders. He said, 'I have sinned by betraying innocent blood.' But they said, 'What is that to us? See to it yourself.' Throwing down the pieces of silver in the temple, he departed; and he went and hanged himself."
Matthew 27:1-5

THEOLOGICAL REFLECTION

Here, we have two people who dealt with the shame of ministry failure in two completely different ways, and the biggest factor affecting this difference is what was in their hearts.

Peter and Judas were both disciples of Jesus Christ, so they had access to Jesus that other people didn't have. They could talk directly to Jesus. They could walk with Him. They could see how our Lord and Savior operated and why He did what He did. In other words, Peter and Judas were two of 12 extraordinarily blessed individuals who had unprecedented access to direct mentorship from Jesus, yet they handled that access in two completely different ways.

When the disciples were first introduced in the narrative in Matthew 10, Peter is named first, and Judas was named last. Of greater theological significance than the order in which these men were listed is the manner in which they were introduced. Peter and the next 10 disciples were simply listed by name, whereas the gospel writer not only lists Judas but also describes his biggest sin. None of the other disciples had their sins put on display like that, especially Peter, who, in publicly denying knowing Him three times, betrayed Jesus, just like Judas did.

So, what was so much worse about the actions of Judas than those of Peter that led to Judas being identified solely by his sin? You could analyze each disciple's moments of betrayal and possibly assert that the betrayal of Judas could be viewed a lot worse than that of Peter because what Judas did led directly to Jesus being crucified. And you wouldn't be wrong in that assertion.

As previously stated, what is more important than what Judas and Peter did is what was in their hearts. Both were flawed individuals, but one's overall motivation for ministry and for life were completely different. Peter had a foul mouth and a quick temper, but he absolutely loved Jesus and would go to bat for Him at any time, which is why he was so heartbroken when he denied Jesus three times, as Jesus said he would.

Judas, on the other hand, may have liked Jesus, and may even have loved Him somewhat, but that love didn't supersede his love for money. So, when Judas realized that the 30 pieces of silver he earned for betraying Jesus couldn't alleviate the pain of knowing he was responsible for His crucifixion, he saw the ultimate vanity in his pursuits and killed himself. He had nothing else to live for.

Because Peter's heart was in the right place, he had everything to live for, and his purpose propelled him forward. Between the resurrection and ascension of Christ, Peter was desperate to show Him how sorry he was for denying Him, how dedicated he was to Him, and how eager he was to preach about Him to the world.

Peter was ashamed of what he did, but his heart and his greater purpose for living overshadowed that shame. Judas had an impure heart, had no greater purpose, had no why, and therefore had nothing but shame, an overpowering shame that caused him to kill himself. And because Judas killed himself, we remember him today for his betrayal. Because Peter continued on in ministry, however, we know him as the rock upon whom the church of Jesus Christ was built.

Two deeply painful betrayals of Christ, two totally different reactions to the shame, two markedly different legacies.

The shame of burning out in ministry is undeniably deep, as you feel like you've let Jesus down and done irreparable harm to your witness. But shame doesn't have to debilitate you. Whether you one day re-enter ministry or not, God still has a plan for your life and is not through with you yet. If you're reading this book right now, my guess is your heart is in the right place, and despite what you've been through, you have a desire to serve God. Let that heart and that desire overpower those feelings of shame so that you can move forward with your life and receive all the blessings God yet has for you.

You show your face again by coming to grips with your humanity, reading the scriptures and remembering you're not the first person (nor will you be the last) to ever falter in ministry, and making the determination that the purpose and plan for your life is yet much greater than the shame and the pain you may be feeling at this moment.

If you don't give up, if you don't give in, your burnout experience won't be the epitaph on your tombstone, but instead, it'll merely be a brief chapter in a beautiful story of a life well lived and a greatness fully realized. You can and you will show your face again because better days are yet ahead.

PRACTICAL APPLICATION

When reflecting on the experiences leading to burnout and the pain of picking up the pieces and attempting to begin again after burnout, it can become very easy to play games with yourself.

The blame game and the shame game.

Previously, I delved further into some of what I went through at my previous church. It was really easy for me to blame myself for things not working out and my resigning from pastoral ministry altogether. I had been a recognized leader in the AME Church, and my future in the denomination as a whole, as well as at my church in particular, was bright. So, for me to last but one year at this charge and to fall in such a public way was definitely a failure in my eyes, and I blamed and second-guessed myself for it for months.

I stopped blaming myself when I finally realized that (1) my appointment to this church placed me in the middle of a generations-long fight that I had nothing to do with, and (2) I was set up in a number of ways to fail from the very beginning and there was nothing I was going to be able to do about it to protect myself other than what I did do—leave.

Shame, however, is a different animal.

As an AME minister, we like to say that ours is a connectional church, meaning that each church is not an entity unto itself, but part of an administrative district, a conference, an Episcopal district, an entire connection. What this means is that not only do we have (oftentimes oppressive) financial obligations to these different entities, but we also have meetings with these groups all throughout the conference year. We probably don't go more than 45 consecutive days without an official AME meeting of some kind.

So, when you have a nasty experience like what I endured, the opportunities for shame are plentiful and the personal feeling of shame is palpable.

A disclaimer

For this reason, dealing with shame may be the one subject related to recovery from pastoral burnout in which I have the least expertise. Nearly two years after my resignation, I'm honestly still dealing with this. I'm still striving earnestly to answer the question, "How do I show my face again?"

A-list blogger, podcaster, and speaker, Michael Hyatt, wrote a fantastic blog post, "5 Reasons You're Not Getting Traction with Your Platform," wherein he states the second reason for this lack of traction is that we don't know what our role as a communicator is [1]. Hyatt states that in platform building, we can communicate from one of three distinct perspectives or positions:

1. The *sage*, a recognized expert in a field with miles of credentials and a voice of authority

2. The *sherpa*, a trusted guide who has had the experience in the area about which he/she is writing and who is now sharing that experience with the voice of confidence and empathy

3. The *struggler*—or, as I like to say, the *sojourner*—who hasn't arrived yet, but is traveling the journey right along with the reader, speaking with the voice of transparency, reporting triumphs and missteps along the way

God blessed me to earn a Doctor of Ministry related to the subject of pastoral burnout, and God has given me a framework for overcoming burnout to share with the world. I am, in many ways, still living this process, however. It's ongoing—for as long as it needs to be.

What I'm sharing regarding shame is the biggest testament to the fact that I am indeed a sojourner. I am no more than two steps ahead of the broken pastor for whom the sting of burnout is fresh, yet I know what God has given me can help. If I can strengthen you through my weakness, if I can build you up through my brokenness, then I've done what I've been called to do.

The permissions in dealing with shame

So, after burnout, how do you deal with shame? How do you show your face again? Doing so requires affording yourself four permissions, four things you must give yourself in order to move past shame to the next step in your rebuilding journey.

1. Give yourself time.

Take as much of it as you need, and then take a little more. Seriously. The first few months after I resigned from pastoral ministry, I had some good colleagues who, out of friendship and brotherhood, gave me the opportunity to minister at their churches. I wasn't looking for preaching engagements at the time, but I definitely appreciated these colleagues for thinking of me. Actually, one of the best sermons I've preached in my entire life came during this valley season.

It wasn't until months later, though, when I was no longer on the forefront of people's minds and the preaching engagements became more infrequent, that I finally had the opportunity to step back for a while, take a break from the church scene, and decompress. I needed this time to heal and regain a kingdom perspective on life and ministry.

2. Give yourself space.

As I stated previously, I am part of a denomination that likes to meet all the time. Going off into a corner and hiding probably would have been much easier had I been part of a more congregational ministry that doesn't get together with other churches as much as AMEs do. I therefore had to stop going to AME meetings, conferences, workshops, and worship services altogether. I don't hate the denomination, but I couldn't put on a smiley face and act like everything was fine between the leadership and myself because it wasn't. It still isn't.

I would be stressing myself out even more if I simply

tried to go to all the same meetings, give hugs, shake hands, and conduct myself as if I had not just been through something traumatic. The colleagues with whom my wife and I were close have loved us even harder since we've been away, even though we don't necessarily see them month after month anymore. They've understood we've needed space. And it's been okay.

3. Give yourself life.

So, how do we as mere human beings give ourselves life when our Father in heaven is the only giver of life? We are instructed in Proverbs 18:21a that "Death and life are in the power of the tongue," meaning we have the power to speak life or death to ourselves, and others have the power to do the same to us. We therefore give ourselves life by doing three things:

Studying the scriptures, committing some of them to memory, and declaring them out loud as often as necessary to build yourself up. My number one scripture in the valley of despair became Psalm 23:5a: "Thou preparest a table before me in the presence of mine enemies…" I repeated it as often as I possibly could and even placed it in my email signature. The promises of God are powerful. They become even more powerful when we commit them to memory, internalize them, personalize them, and release them into the atmosphere.

Associating with individuals who will affirm what's in you, rather than what happened to you. Job really needed his friends to minister to him and encourage him back to vitality, but all they did was make him feel even worse about himself and about his God. And his wife, his helpmeet, didn't make it any better. Yes, we all need mentors to push us into greater, as well as colleague-friends to support us professionally in that effort, but we need, just as much, if not more so, at least one close friend with whom you can be yourself and share candidly, as this person knows you better than anyone, far beyond your position, your title, and your past.

Consuming affirming media. By affirming media, I don't

mean explicitly Christian material, but books and other audio and video material that can speak to you in your present state and both challenge and encourage you to aim higher. For instance, I'm a voracious podcast consumer. Any time I'm not working or spending time with the family, I'm listening to hours and hours daily of podcasts that either entertain me or, specific to this point, educate me and/or challenge me to think critically, look at the world differently, and take action to achieve my goals. Not every podcast that does this is hosted by a Christian. I'm willing to listen to anything, regardless of the faith tradition of the source, as long as what they espouse adds value to my life and is communicated in a respectful, non-blasphemous manner. Anything that challenges you to be the best possible version of yourself is affirming.

4. Give yourself a dose of reality.

I'd be remiss were I not honest with you here. The truth of the matter is you may never fully get past some of the things you endured during your burnout experience. You may never mend some of the broken relationships along the way. You may never again fellowship with some of the same people. But you have to get to the point where all of that is okay.

Just because these things may never happen again doesn't mean you don't forgive and move on; you absolutely must do that. The experience of pastoral burnout is a traumatic one, however, and to think that somehow you'll be able to go back to the way things used to be is asking a lot of your heart. Such is a work of regeneration that only the Holy Spirit can accomplish, and if that happens, know there's a greater purpose in it than what's been revealed to you at this point.

Giving yourself a break

In total, you show your face again after burnout by being real with yourself and realizing that (a) there is no shame in having struggles in ministry, and (b) you have the space and time to react like a real human being in the face of trauma.

There is no shame in ministry struggles because we're out to win souls for Christ. That's not supposed to be easy. Just like Job wasn't allowed to simply live piously without experiencing loss and being thus tested to the full extent of his faith, we should not expect to bring great glory to Christ without great struggle. Also, just because we purport ourselves to be spiritual people doesn't mean we're not going to face the full gamut of humanity in how we process what we've been through. There's nothing wrong with that.

Once we have dealt with these issues, we'll never again have to feel ashamed to be around other people. While we may never "get over it," we will have better days, and the four permissions will help us to no longer be prisoners of shame.

DEVOTIONAL POINTS

Reflect

1. Think about everything you've ever done wrong in ministry. Get angry about your supposed failure, and get sad about what could have been. Process those memories and emotions. Then, give them all over to Jesus, let Him heal you, and be encouraged, knowing the fact that you're still breathing means God is not through with you yet.

2. Recall everything Peter did in the book of Acts to build the first-century Christian Church, and think about the fact that he never would have been able to do any of that had he allowed his shame to overtake him as it did Judas.

Read

1. 1. Matthew 27, John 21.
2. Blog post, "Stressed Out Pastors, Crazy Sins, and the Death of Pastor Zach Tims," by prominent writer, life coach, humanitarian, activist, and former pastor, Shaun King [2]. As a one who experienced burnout in pastoral ministry, Shaun has several posts on his blog related to burnout, but this one in particular was worth highlighting in this context, not necessarily because it deals the shame of burnout but

because of the pain that comes from the shameful things Zachery Tims, the wildly popular pastor Shaun was writing about, was doing before his tragic passing in 2011. The pain and shame of burning out in ministry and feeling like a failure is not entirely different from the shame many pastors who operate at a high level in public have because of the things they've done in private. In either case, that pain and shame can be overcome, and the solutions Shaun offers in the post are highly relevant to burnout recovery.

Pray
#PrayForYourPastor
Your pastor may or may not have skeletons he or she is fighting to keep in the closet. Either way, your pastor needs your daily prayers. Vocational ministry is very difficult work, and the internal and external pressures of the job can lead to a leader's physical and/or spiritual breakdown that could cause burnout. Rally together with your fellow laypersons to create the kind of church atmosphere that helps a pastor work to the best of his or her ability. Pray that your pastor has a support system that will keep him or her humble, accountable, grounded, and sane. And if you ever do learn something unfavorable about your pastor, pray for him or her even harder that God's grace would abound until eradication of whatever that unfavorable thing is takes place. Your pastor needs you!

My prayer for you…
Father, in Jesus' name, your servants are in need of your care like never before. They are being weighed down by the shame of burning out in ministry, and that shame is holding them back from moving forward with life. Let your servants know you are not angry and have not left their side. Encourage them, Father, and give reassurance that better days, better seasons are yet ahead. Remove every person, every environment, every spirit from your servants' lives that would reinforce a negative mindset. Connect your servants

with positive resources and positive people who will affirm the best parts of who they are, while giving grace to those parts that aren't as good. I ask these things in the name of Jesus, Amen.

Shame

II
REBUILD YOUR FOUNDATION

After rebuilding the psyche and getting mental faculties in order, the recovering pastor's foundation must be rebuilt. The man or woman of God needs to rediscover the essence of who he or she is outside of the pastorate, beyond the pulpit, without the title or position. What was life like before the recovering pastor became a pastor? Since a pastor can easily lose himself or herself over years of unyielding loyalty to the ministry and to the people of God, it is critically important for him or her to reconnect to the aspects of his or her personality or life in general that aren't entirely related to ministry because those are what will endure, whether the recovering pastor one day reenters vocational ministry or not.

CYLAR

-4-
FAMILY
Your first ministry

"He must manage his own household well, keeping his children submissive and respectful in every way—for if someone does not know how to manage his own household, how can he take care of God's church?"
1 Timothy 3:4-5

THEOLOGICAL REFLECTION

It is not easy to find a strong biblical reference to support the belief that one's family is his or her very first ministry. This directive from Paul in his first letter to Timothy is the only of its kind in the Bible. In discussing ministry to the family, various verses in Proverbs and other scriptures about children honoring their parents are referenced, along with the all too familiar instructions from Paul to the Ephesians about wives submitting to their husbands and husbands loving their wives as Christ loved the church (Ephesians 5:22-33).

What you'll commonly find in scripture are examples of men consistently failing their families in the Old Testament, the apostles forsaking all to follow Christ and therefore not having families of their own because of the weight of their callings, wives being told to submit, and children being told to obey. But Paul's question of how one can handle the affairs of the church without first maintaining a stable household expresses an idea not prevalent throughout the word of God.

The problem with Paul's directive, though, is that we find it in the midst of controversial passages about the role of women in the home and in ministry. It is easy to allow an important conversation about the role of family in ministry to be co-opted by sexism, so some explanation is in order here.

When Paul is instructing Timothy about the qualifications for one to become a bishop, the apostle uses masculine pronouns throughout, which is consistent with his previous teaching in his first letter to Timothy (1 Tim 2:9-15) and in earlier epistles, such as the aforementioned letter to the Ephesians and his first letter to the church at Corinth (1 Cor 14:34-36). Paul's teachings in these various scriptures comprise some of the more controversial passages in the Bible because they are commonly used to subordinate the woman in ministry.

Some contextual analysis, however, with the help of biblical commentaries and other references, reveals there were some specific issues taking place with specific women acting and speaking irresponsibly in some of the places Paul was overseeing, so much of what Paul is teaching is not speaking to women universally but to a particular group of women, based on the issues of that time.

While some denominations in the 21st century and beyond continue to hold fast to the literal teaching of Paul and assert that either women are not called to preach at all or that they simply cannot be bishops in the Lord's church, many denominations do have women throughout their ecclesiastical structure, all the way up to the bishopric. I am of the latter camp and am actually married to a woman in ministry. If we consider each of the gospel narratives (Matt 28:8 | Mark 16:8 | Luke 24:9-11 | John 20:2), we will find women were actually the first preachers of the gospel, running from the empty tomb to share with the disciples the good news of Jesus being raised from the dead. And we can look back to the book of Judges and observe the powerful leadership of the prophetess Deborah (Jdg 4-5) as an example of a woman in spiritual leadership over men.

With that said, Paul's question to Timothy is spot on. How can someone take care of God's church if he or she cannot take care of the home? If one's ministry has not had any effect on his or her spouse or children, can we expect that ministry to positively affect the people of God? The manner in which the people who are closest to you, the people who live in your house and have contact with you every day think and act on a daily basis is a reflection of what is happening in your life. God is not going to just bless one person in a household and leave everyone else out; if God has a word for the house, it's for everyone in that house. If we forsake our families to do the work of ministry, we're not truly doing the work of ministry, for as the old cliché goes, charity begins at home.

It is critically important for one who is in ministry to actually do the work of ministry, attending to and caring for the people and the programs of the church. For the burnt-out pastor, doing the work was likely not the issue. With 80 percent of pastors believing ministry has negatively affected their family, it's more likely the bigger problem was properly balancing church and home life. Meeting the never-ending demands of a pastor's church family and those of the greater community, it is very easy to see how his or her family could feel neglected, especially in a local church context wherein that pastor has not fully delegated ministry responsibility to a hired or volunteer staff.

If your family life was lacking during your pastorate, pray fervently that God will warm the hearts of your spouse and children as you reconcile with them and move forward. If you were indeed faithful to your family, however, yet still experienced burnout, be encouraged because you now have the advantage of knowing your spouse and your children will be there to encourage you and lift you back up to a place of usefulness and productivity in life. Either way, you need your family now more than ever as you begin putting your life back together again. The foundation of the burnt-out pastor is the family, the people who know, love, and appreciate you beyond your title, beyond your position. For just as charity begins at home, so does the process of rebuilding your life and ministry.

PRACTICAL APPLICATION

I am a workaholic. My wife will tell you that without hesitation. I've spent more than a few movie nights, mall trips, weekend afternoons, and other blocks of typical recreation time in my office, chipping away at the vision God has given me, positioning myself to fulfill the mandate that has been spoken over me.

But let me tell you, there's no greater joy than coming home every evening to my ladies. I have no clue what I would do without my wife and my two crazy daughters. I truly believe without them, the events that led to my burnout would have absolutely destroyed me. I may not even have survived to share my experiences.

What I went through ate away at my very soul, day after painful day, but coming home to my family made things just a little more bearable.

During my tenure at this church, Steward Board and Trustee Board meetings were scheduled at 6pm on the second and third Tuesdays every month, respectively. By November of that year, just my third month there, enough negativity had already been stirred up throughout the church that it bubbled over into both of these meetings.

We got about 15 minutes into the agenda in both meetings before the criticisms started to fly like projectiles launched in my direction. For three hours—90 minutes the second Tuesday of November and another 90 minutes the third Tuesday—I let every single officer of that church speak their mind without interruption or comment from me.

Afterward, each time, I said a few words, adjourned the meeting, then put on my jacket, picked up my bag, walked straight out the door to my car, and promptly drove straight home without a word to anyone.

One criticism no one can ever make about me is that I was not open to feedback and not willing to entertain conversation with people who had critical things to say about me. I consider self-awareness and openness to growth two of my greatest qualities. My supporters—my wife included—will tell you I was too willing to be criticized. They'll tell you I should have never allowed that to happen.

Well, I allowed it, I sat through it, and I took my criticism like a man. But I'd be lying if I said these words didn't take a tremendous toll on my spirit. That third Tuesday in November was particularly hard because some of the members of that Trustee Board were among the coldest, meanest people I've met in my entire life, and I could feel their nasty spirits radiating onto mine.

The hour-long commute home that night was equally painful, as I called my wife and recounted everything that had happened, but when I made it into my garage, parked my car, and walked inside my door, my oldest daughter gave me a hero's welcome, suitable for a soldier returning home from combat. My youngest was not yet three months old at the time, so she couldn't come greet me herself, but I was definitely glad to see her, especially after all the love her big sister had just given me.

Coming home after a tough day of work and being able to lay my eyes on my beautiful babies meant everything to me. The people's negative spirits broke me down, but my girls' warm spirits built me back up. My girls didn't care about titles, budgets, deadlines, who said what, who did what, or whose ego did or did not get stroked. All they cared about was that daddy was home.

The love of God was made manifest in the hearts of my baby girls. How could I ever give that up? Family first.

A non-negotiable

Previously, I shared just a few of countless situations that occurred at my last church that should have been clear indications to me that things were not going to work out there, as much as I wanted them to.

One such instance I neglected to share was an exchange I had in my office one morning with my most critical member.

Aside: This most critical member was a thorn in my side from day one and was chiefly responsible for a lot of the mess I went through during my short tenure there. The one positive thing she did do, however, that many other detractors did not do was she actually had the courage to come to my office and air her grievances. She neither did it respectfully—I should have kicked her out of my office plenty of times—nor out of love, but at least she did it. Going through a firestorm is stressful enough. Don't allow yourself to be more stressed by people who don't even have enough decency to treat you like an adult, look you in the eye, and tell you what they think of you.

This member, like many others, didn't like the fact that I was so dedicated to my family, and she showed a complete lack of understanding of or concern for the unique circumstances I was in regarding welcoming another child into the world at the same time as beginning a new pastoral charge in a new city. One particular comment this member made about my family involvement one day really bothered me:

"Pastor, as you get older and further into your career, you'll realize at times, you have to do what you have to do, and family is not always going to come first. We've all been there."

What she said severely bothered me because it came from a really bad place. The comment, in a vacuum, wasn't really an issue. I fully understand there are seasons in all of our lives where we have to put some things off to the side, re-prioritize our chief obligations, and burn the candle on both ends to get things done and finish our biggest projects.

There are times I don't get to spend all the time I want with my wife and kids, but to the point of complete neglect for the sake of the gospel? No. I'm not doing that. That's a value decision I've made repeatedly throughout my ministry, but I know that's not necessarily the same for everybody, so, on its own, I understand the statement.

I knew this most critical member was making her comments from a really bad, condescending place because she knew all I had already been through and was still dealing with concerning my family at the time, yet she still felt she needed to make it a point to tell me about my priorities.

Furthermore, what made the "as you get older...further" quip worse to me was the fact that during my time at the helm, she never hesitated to let me know she was the longest-tenured member of the church. She wore it as a badge of honor. And because she had been at the church longer than any other member, she felt that longevity gave her the right to teach me, this little ol' 30 year-old boy (Yes, she absolutely did call me that in a meeting one day) how to balance my time as a professional.

From the beginning of my pastorate, I made a promise to my wife that I would never forsake her or our future children to advance in ministry, and I was true to that promise all the way. To me, it just didn't make any sense for me to cast the people I loved the most to the side in order to bend over backwards for people who would either (a) love me one minute and leave me the next, or (b) never have any respect for me, no matter what I did.

It would have been foolhardy for me to let the people who loved me unconditionally falter because I spent all my time with people who not only didn't love me, but had all kinds of conditions. Conditions I'd never be able to fulfill.

How I prioritized my family life was a non-negotiable.

I still had some work to do

I love my wife. I love my daughters. After God, of course, they are numbers 2, 2a, and 2b in my life. I'd be nothing without them, and I try to let them know that as often as I possibly can.

And I'm not just saying this because it sounds good, because it appears virtuous to be a hardworking man who loves his family. I can write these words with the highest degree of integrity because I've backed them up all throughout my ministry.

To a fault, depending on who you ask.

But when I stepped down from pastoral ministry, even with how I prioritized my family life, even with how unapologetic I was about being a family man, I still had some issues to reconcile. After my burnout experience, I still had to refocus on my family in certain areas.

My wife was as broken as I was, if not more so. My children had erratic sleep patterns because of all the traveling from conference to conference and back and forth from our home to the parsonage next to the church. Our house was in disarray after moving everything back home from the parsonage and doing some remodeling afterward.

Focusing on what's important

My resignation from pastoral ministry was the end of a chapter in my life, but by the same token, in more ways than one, it was really just the beginning of this burnout journey. After experiencing burnout, I had to take a number of steps to rebuild my life and put myself back together again. One such step in the rebuilding process was learning to refocus on my family; I had to do this in five ways.

1. I had to let my wife know she wasn't the enemy.

I have no problem sharing that during my fifth and final year of pastoring, I got into a lot of fights with my wife. Neither of us were physically or verbally abusive toward one another, but we had several heated discussions that year, and some regrettable things were said. The vast majority of them were on my end.

My wife has been nothing but an encourager to me in everything I've done since we've known each other. In ministry, she's never hindered me, but she's truly helped me every step of the way. In fact, her heart for the people, her ministry experience, and a number of other skills she brings to the table help to pick me up in the areas where I'm weak.

And not only that, but she's my best friend. I can talk to her, and I know she's not judging me. If I say something crazy, I know she's going to call me out on it because she loves me enough to tell me what I need to hear, not what I want to hear. She has my best interests at heart in every situation and is always ready to fight anyone or anything on my behalf, even when I don't want her to.

But during my year from ministry hell, I didn't show her any of this appreciation, not because I forgot how much she meant to me, but because I had allowed the cares of this world and the troubles of ministry to take me so far to the edge that I no longer knew how to talk to her lovingly.

I would come home from a tough day of work and find myself in arguments with her over absolutely nothing because I was wound so tight with the stress of doing business day to day at this church. I was on the edge so much that my wife, the one who's always had my back, became the enemy.

Even after leaving the pastorate, it took a bit of time for me to get the edge out of my voice and the animosity out of my heart so I could actually carry on a decent conversation with my wife. Even though she was very understanding and knew I didn't consider her the enemy, it was very much necessary for me to tell her that so she could feel comfortable talking to me without anticipating my blowing up at her.

2. I had to stop talking about ministry at home.

When I stepped down from the pastorate, my daily conversation still revolved around the church for several weeks because (a) all the hurt and pain from the previous 12 months was still fresh in my mind, (b) I met some fairly intense opposition in trying to handle some unfinished business matters on my way out of the church, and (c) we still had a small contingent of wonderful friends from the church who we still did life with, as prominent podcaster and life and business coach Cliff Ravenscraft would say [1].

Despite these various factors that still kept the church relevant in our lives, I had to stop talking about the church at home. The only way I was going to get healing from my involvement with that church, the only way I was going to heal our marriage and have a decent conversation with my wife was that I simply had to stop talking about anything having to do with the church.

Not only was it unwise and unhealthy to keep bombarding my wife with every negative feeling that would bubble up in my spirit during the healing process, but quite frankly, there were other things in life to talk about. Continuing to focus all of my attention on one aspect of my life, as pervasive as it was, was simply shrinking my world, and I wasn't going to let that continue to happen.

3. I had to let my children know Daddy was available.

Candace, my precious firstborn, is a genius. She is especially gifted with associations. My wife and brother in law recall an instance a couple years ago, before Candace even turned 2, when she reached into the recycle bin we had in our kitchen pantry, pulled out an empty bottle of extra strength 5-hour energy, and exclaimed "Daddy!"

She also imitates everything I do, so every time I'm in my home office working, she will pull up one of her small chairs next to me and start banging away on a keyboard to an old computer because, as she proudly tells her mother or anyone who asks her what she's doing, "I'm working like Daddy!"

I don't want Candace or her younger sister, Jada, to always associate me with energy drinks, computer screens, and keyboards. I need them to understand I'm available for playtime because I don't want them to grow up thinking I wasn't there for them and that Daddy was nothing but a workaholic. I need them to know I'm always paying attention to them and am proud of them.

When I was going through the fire, it was hard for me to break away from my work because the pressures of just trying to maintain and trying to please people who didn't like me were great. Survival, not bringing glory to Christ through my ministry, became my chief motivation, so I didn't have any balance in my life. But now that I'm in a better place spiritually, and especially since I've completed my DMin studies, I am able to enjoy my children much more than I used to.

4. As good as my wife is at handling the children, I had to learn to jump in more often.

My wife is so good with our girls. When they are hurt, sick, or simply upset, she knows just what to say or do to get them back to 100 percent. Things I'm just not good at doing.

But she has a life, too. She has clients, projects, friends, and outside interests, just like I do, so I've had to make more of a concerted effort to jump in and do more with the girls so she can take care of what she needs to do.

Admittedly, this is something I'm still working on. I help as much as I can with potty time, bath time, administering medicine when necessary, and no matter what I'm doing, I always help with bed time, but I could still do more. I don't make their doctors appointments or keep up with their medical records—she's better at that than I am—and I don't do much cooking, not because I can't (ask her about my lasagna), but I have so many irons on the fire right now with other projects, and I haven't taken the time to truly go to work in the kitchen like I know I can.

5. I had to help my children love church again.

Before my year from hell, I spent four great years in Windsor, Ontario, Canada pastoring a people we had grown to love very much and who loved us. We still keep in contact with many of them today.

They were such great members because they actually allowed my wife and me to lead them, as we had built up a high level of trust with them over the years, and they knew that the vision God had given me was something they could connect with confidently.

We didn't have a lot of instrumentation there—a piano player and occasionally, a drummer—but we had open, authentic, powerful worship experiences. Candace had also grown to love the people and love the worship. She even had a favorite song, "Jesus, Jesus, Jesus":

*Jesus Jesus Jesus, there's just
something about that name.
Master, Saviour, Jesus, like the
fragrance after the rain
Jesus, Jesus, Jesus, let all heaven and
earth proclaim
Kings and kingdoms will pass away
But there's something about that Name!*

Candace loved going to church and looked forward to it every week. I know this because she would get excited about it and ask, "Daddy, are we going to church today?" or "Daddy, can we go to church?" Jada, on the other hand, didn't get to experience this because we were transferred out of Canada two days before she was born.

Things were not so pleasant at the new church. I think Candace intuitively understood Daddy was having problems there, and it didn't sit well with her. Also, people weren't willing to admit this, but the church wasn't as welcoming to young people as it could have been. The people said they were, but their actions said otherwise, and the youth picked up on it. I know because they would come to me and share their frustrations with me personally.

I think my daughter picked up on it, too. One day, out of nowhere, she said very plainly that she didn't want to go to church. Of course, she went anyway because she had to, but she wasn't happy about it and cried at a point in the service because she was so upset.

When we left the church, it took a while for Candace to take an interest in church again, and when she finally did, Jada did, as well. Jada had not experienced what it meant to be in a loving church environment, so when she did, she liked it.

If it were up to my wife and me, we could have simply stayed home on Sundays and not been bothered with the local church for a long, long time, but we felt it was important to be somewhere, not necessarily as members, but just somewhere we could worship freely and seek respite during our season of recovery and transition. We found that place, and the girls are happy about it.

And that makes me happy.

I am nothing without my family; I will say that until my dying day. That is why I absolutely had to take some tangible steps to refocus on my family after the burnout experience. Like other points in my rebuilding process, this refocusing is certainly a work in progress, but it's a work I'll never give up on. It's too important.

DEVOTIONAL POINTS
Reflect

1. Think back to the day you got married. In fact, if you know you married the right one, you ought to be able to reach back for the memory of when you first fell in love. How did you feel?

2. Do you remember how you felt the day your children were born? Your children's date(s) of birth and your wedding day ought to be two of the best days of your life. Hold on to these memories for strength and encouragement as you lean into your family in this rebuilding season.

3. What you've been through or are currently going through has been deeply painful and therefore stays top-of-mind all the time. Think about who else you can share that pain with other than your spouse, though, not because you should ever keep anything from your spouse, but because he or she is likely already fatigued from witness, hearing, and talking about what you've been through. You need to heal, but your spouse does, too. Prayerfully, you have someone else or a group of people you can talk to about some of these

issues.
Read
1. 1 Timothy 2-3; Galatians 5; 1 Corinthians 11, 15
2. Blog post, "How to Be an Ephesians 5 Husband for Your Proverbs 31 Wife," by family leadership blogger Jackie Bledsoe, Jr. on BlackandMarriedWithKids.com [2]. This wonderful article presents a fresh, non-sexist perspective on the role of the man in a Christian household. Men and women will appreciate this one!

Pray
#PrayForYourPastor

Your pastor needs prayer concerning his or her family life. Pray that God would remove every obstacle limiting his or her family time and that the Holy Spirit would reveal to your pastor things that can be done, systems and processes that can be implemented, and even volunteers who can step up to enhance the ministry, get the most out of every minute he or she must spend at the church, and maximize the time he or she can spend at home. Pray even harder for your pastor's spouse and children. Pray that God would grant them the strength to withstand the attack of the enemy on their household that would try to distract them and your pastor from doing the work of kingdom building.

Pray also for the courage to lovingly but boldly confront anyone, church member or not, who would (a) seek to publicly or privately denigrate your pastor and his or her family in any way, or (b) make your pastor feel guilty for desiring to spend more time with his or her family. And if you have been that person in the past, pray for God to cleanse your heart, and schedule a meeting with your pastor to iron out any issue that would prevent you from serving him or her to the best of your ability (of course, in the bounds of what is appropriate in your walk with God).

My prayer for you...

In Jesus' name, I pray, Lord, that you would help your

broken servants to refocus on their families in this season of transition. If your servants were not faithful to their household, warm the hearts of spouse and children to forgive, detangle the lines of communication, and rebuild the bridges of trust between everyone in the home so that all can move forward with life, whether in or outside of ministry.

If they did actually prioritize their family life in a balanced way and spouse and children know that to be true, strengthen them to be an encouragement to your servants in this time of need. Bring back to your servants' memory all the good times shared with their family, and may those memories form a healing balm for your servants' very soul, providing the assurance that they are loved, valued, cared about, and appreciated, for knowing these things will tremendously help your servants rebuild and be whole again. I ask this all in the name of Jesus the Christ, Amen.

Family

-5-
COMMUNITY
Because we all need each other
"Iron sharpens iron,
and one person sharpens the wits of another."
Proverbs 27:17

THEOLOGICAL REFLECTION

Solomon's wisdom in this particular proverb is very rich. Upon first glance, it is not difficult to see the main idea here is that we are supposed to have people in our lives who not just encourage us, but also hold us accountable and challenge us to be the best version of ourselves that we can possibly be.

What is deeper here is Solomon's imagery of the two pieces of iron. Whether you're in ministry or law, medicine, education, athletics, entertainment, or any professional field, the concept is universal. You are a piece of iron that needs another piece of iron to sharpen you and make you better. No matter how strong or sharp you start out, no matter how powerful your ministry is, regardless of how far your anointing takes you or how much room your gifts make for you, you are going to need sharpening at some point in time, and you're going to need another piece of iron to do that sharpening.

Iron can't be sharpened by brick, nor will a piece of wood do the trick. You are iron, and you need more iron to make you better.

Whatever your field of human endeavor, you need a fellow sojourner, someone who can identify with your triumphs and challenges, your strengths and weaknesses, your good days and bad days. You need to build community specifically with people who are or have been where you are professionally, who understand the nuances specific to your industry, and who can speak to you very directly about those particular challenges. Iron sharpening iron is especially key in ministry because as a pastor, you want to feel comfortable discussing congregational leadership challenges with others who are similarly leading congregations, just as CEOs join mastermind groups to discuss issues and ideas with fellow CEOs, not employees.

Iron sharpening iron is even more key for the burnt-out pastor because it is likely that he or she was lonely in the first place, which might possibly have been one of the factors leading to burnout. Yes, the burnout has taken place, but it's not too late. In fact, it's more important now than ever.

As the burnt-out pastor rebuilds his or her life, he or she may be dealing with intense loneliness, and because of possible feelings of shame, as discussed previously, it is critically important that he or she finds a community of other former or current pastors who may have dealt with burnout at any point in their ministries. Being able to have one's iron sharpened by others who have gone through the fire can be life-changing for the rebuilding pastor, providing the encouragement necessary to pick him/herself up, dust him/herself off, and putting his or her life back together again in a spiritually healthy way.

Satan can make God's servants feel they are on individual islands all by themselves, but the power of community, authentic Christian community, will break the chains of isolationism and endow broken leaders with the strength to get started again.

Next to the word of God, the sharpest, most powerful weapon against the attack of the enemy is the cloud of witnesses, the fellowship of the saints. Just as Elijah realized in 1 Kings 19:19, the amount of strength that comes from just knowing we are not alone is immeasurable. Community encourages us, community strengthens us, community heals us, community rebuilds us. Community gives us the blessed assurance of knowing we aren't the first person to ever endure what we've been through, and we certainly won't be the last.

PRACTICAL APPLICATION

Any burnout experience, whether in ministry, or in business, or in interpersonal relationships, or even in physical activity, we all get to that point where we realize and say to ourselves, "Enough is enough!" And even after we've removed ourselves from that situation for a season, we should all be able to look back to a certain point in that ordeal and remember exactly what that breaking point was.

That point for me was the beginning of June 2013, during an under-supported, poorly attended Men's Day revival that many purposely decided to stay home from merely because I had planned it. I had fully realized that my tenure at this church would last no longer than one painfully short year. The day I had this final realization was the first night of the three-day revival.

I cried. Then, I prayed, had a pep talk with my wife, and decided to stick it out the rest of the conference year and finish strong. I survived this most difficult season of my life and was able to write the words you're reading right now because God kept me for the purpose of using my burnout experience to help pull as many pastors as I can out of theirs.

What I was lacking

I did have some colleagues who knew what I was going through let me know they supported me and to reach out and give them a call if I ever wanted to talk. I appreciated the sentiment, but (a) talking on the phone to people other than my wife and closest friends is not necessarily my thing, and

(b) it's not always wise or even safe to share your business with colleagues from the same denomination, reporting to the same leadership and oftentimes ministering to the same people.

My closest friends aren't pastors and therefore could only identify so much with what I was going through. Also, while my wife is my best friend, the daughter of a pastor, and herself a preacher who definitely could identify with my struggles, bringing so much of the church drama home with me on a nightly basis was as hard on my wife as it was on me and certainly took its toll on our marriage.

I needed an ecumenical, supportive, non-judgmental network of pastors who could help me through this most difficult season of my life, not because I think it would've changed my status at the church, but because it might have helped me avoid depression in the midst of the storm.

I needed community, but it turns out I needed to step down from full-time vocational ministry to find it.

The project my pain produced

My lifeline and my saving grace from throwing in the towel and giving up completely on ministry and on God was that I still had work to do. That work was finishing my Doctor of Ministry program, which I had begun a year and a half prior to my resignation from the pastorate, while I was flying high as the youngest Presiding Elder in African Methodism.

When I entered the DMin program at Ecumenical Theological Seminary, I knew I wanted to study the role of social media in building community and spiritual formation, but the actual ministry event I was going to create as the vehicle for my study was much different than how it actually turned out.

The way in which I vacated my position made it virtually impossible to involve any AME colleagues in my project, as I had initially planned. I therefore had to make some major changes and involve an ecumenical group of participants. The biggest changes I was forced to make to my project, however, were to the scope and focus thereof.

I used targeted LinkedIn groups to recruit an interdenominational, intergenerational, multiethnic, multinational group of 14 volunteers to participate for two months in an online community of current or former pastors who had experienced burnout at any point in their ministries. The participant pool was broad enough to include as many perspectives and viewpoints as possible, while keeping the subject focus narrowly niched for greater relevancy.

Our primary mode of interaction was through the forums page on a private membership website I had created specifically for the project [1]. On these forums, we shared our candid perspectives on five bi-weekly discussion questions relevant to community building and burnout in pastoral ministry. I also created a private Facebook group and scheduled Google Hangout videoconferencing to supplement this interaction.

Project takeaways

We learned a lot about each other throughout these two months and encouraged each other through the brutally honest sharing of our burnout experiences. Although some of us were further along in the process than others, everyone who earnestly participated and committed to getting something out of the project reported having benefited because of their involvement.

The research question my ministry event was designed to answer was: "What are the characteristics and benefits of an online pastoral support group in a social media setting?" The most significant characteristic of an online pastoral support group, as shared by the participants who agreed to an exit interview, was a comfortable environment for candid sharing, supported by an expectation of and mutual respect for each other's privacy. The most significant benefit reported was that of encouragement through shared story to continue in ministry.

For me personally, having the opportunity to do this project and glean wisdom from the similar experiences of an ecumenical group of pastoral colleagues encouraged me beyond measure, giving me the assurance that there indeed was life after burnout and that there was yet plenty of kingdom work to do, whether I one day reentered vocational ministry or not.

We all learned a great deal, but I can confidently assert no one took away more from this experience than I did, not just because I was the researcher, but because I was in such desperate need of community before the project began. Going from the high of being the youngest in an entire denomination to serve in my position to the depths of despair of burning out and resigning from a new charge after just one year was beyond depressing.

The gift of purpose

I was down in the dumps, doubting my call and questioning my very purpose in life when I resigned from pastoral ministry. But God thought enough of me to not allow me to sit idle and wallow in my depression. God looked out for me and sent a group of brothers in ministry, most of whom were strangers, to minister to me through this project in unspeakable ways.

Finishing this DMin project gave me my hope back. It helped to restore my sense of purpose and passion for ministry. I'm not totally "over" everything I endured during my burnout experience, but I can honestly say I am whole again. All is not right with the individuals in authority over me in this situation—it probably will never be—but it doesn't have to be for me to move on.

And move on is exactly what I've done. I may never pastor again. I don't desire to, at all. But I have a heart and a newfound passion for encouraging and helping to restore pastors to a place of usefulness and vitality in the world, whether that place is inside or outside of the pulpit. I will write books, speak in multiple venues, create educational material, and build community around this passion. I will also support the efforts of people like Bo Lane with ExPastors.com and all others in the kingdom who are doing the same thing.

Through this experience, God revealed a greater purpose for my life and ministry than I had ever conceived of before. When I burned out and my passion for ministry left me, my purpose in ministry, revealed through my DMin studies, kept me.

Have you ever lost a loved one and attempted to keep busy in order to deaden the sting of the mourning season? I've surely been there. But in this case, staying busy actually helped me to mourn and guided me down the path toward deliverance and recovery from burnout. I thank and praise God.

Your purpose will keep you when your passion leaves you. And then, sooner or later, your passion returns, marries your purpose, and manifests one hundredfold in your life, reawakening within you your reason for living, and giving you a community of people who share your heart, who have your back, and who will encourage and strengthen you to live out that reason. It's a beautiful thing.

DEVOTIONAL POINTS

Reflect

1. Honestly answer these questions for yourself: Do I have anyone (besides my spouse, who could probably use a break at times from all of my sharing) I can talk to about what I'm going through? We all have different journeys, but we have some similar experiences along the way—Do I have anyone in my life who can identify with my experiences and encourage me in Christ to be the best me I can be?

2. Have I sat down and listened to anyone else's problems (only as much as you're able to handle) and attempted to be a source of encouragement for them? We can often encourage ourselves by listening to others' stories and encouraging them. Our blessing could be right in the middle

of our ministry to others.

Read
1. 1 Kings 19. If you can get your hands on a HarperCollins NRSV Study Bible, even just the commentary for this chapter will bless you tremendously.
2. *Think and Grow Rich* by Napoleon Hill. This book has been a staple in business and entrepreneurship for generations, and one of the concepts for which the book is most significant and relevant in the 21st century is that of mastermind groups. This book will provide some additional practical application of the principles shared in this chapter.
3. ExPastors.com, founded by Bo Lane, author of *Why Pastors Quit* (read that, too). For the past four years, Bo has curated a wealth of resources, including videos, articles, books, and blog posts from him and from a number of guest bloggers that speak directly to pastors who have left ministry and are looking to begin life again. Reading the blog posts, especially those from the guest bloggers, as well as the comments on those posts, are very comforting because even though what they're talking about at times can be extremely sad, it's encouraging to know that God is still working in these posters, despite what they've been through. The statistics on burnout in pastoral ministry are ubiquitous, but it's when you hear the stories and meet the people behind those statistics that those numbers come alive and you truly begin to realize just how common your experiences are, as bad as they hurt. The more you can connect with others who identify with your story, the better.

Pray
#PrayForYourPastor

Just as your pastor needs to get away sometimes to spend time with his or her family, he or she also needs to find community, especially with colleagues outside of your denomination, organization, or fellowship. Pray that your pastor is able to find people he or she can communicate with on a regular basis to keep him or her sane, encouraged, and hopeful for the future.

Pray earnestly and fervently that your pastor is able to find this group, whether online or offline, and fellowship with them as often as possible, not so he or she can gossip about you, but so his or her iron can be sharpened by sojourners in ministry who will affirm the anointing of God within your pastor and remind him or her that God is still with him or her, no matter what's happening. The sooner your pastor can find a group like this and the more often he or she can fellowship with this group, the more effective, the more compassionate, the stronger, the wiser, the better your pastor will be in the long term. We all need each other, and your pastor needs people, too. Pray for that to happen.

My prayer for you…

Father, in the name of Jesus, I pray for your lonely, burnt-out servants who did the work of ministry to the best of their ability, but didn't have anyone to share ideas, struggles, and frustrations with along the way. Your children had plans and ideas for the future, but were unable to get the unbiased professional opinion of anyone outside of their denomination to help in those endeavors. Your servants ran into trouble with the people and programs of the church and didn't have anyone they could talk to and share those burdens confidentially. Now that they suffered burnout, those feelings of loneliness, isolation, and frustration are likely greater than ever before.

My prayer, Lord, is that you would send people into your servants' lives who would minister to them and give them some comfort in knowing that those experiences that led to burnout are common, but can be overcome. God, help build your servants back up again through community. Allow them to find community through an online or offline group that will listen to, empathize with, challenge, uplift, and encourage them to rebuild and recover to a place of usefulness and vitality in the kingdom of God. May this community you introduce into your servants' lives be the healing balm they need to start putting the broken pieces back together again. Please, Lord, allow your rebuilding servant to know, in no uncertain terms, that you have not forgotten about and are looking out for them. In Jesus' name, Amen.

-6-
BALANCE
More than just your position
"They love to have the place of honor at banquets and the best seats in the synagogues…"
Matthew 23:6

THEOLOGICAL REFLECTION

The Bible, from Genesis through Revelation, in all of its accounts, histories, dramatic narrations, laws, parables, and prophetic messages, is essentially one story of a perfect God redeeming an imperfect, broken, depraved people through the person of Jesus Christ. Therefore, the act of discovering or rediscovering hobbies and interests outside of ministry does not receive extensive theological treatment, as such is not the point of scripture.

What we do see, however, is the importance of balance in every area of the Christian life. We see Solomon wisely allude to that balance in the very familiar third chapter of Ecclesiastes, when he famously declares there is a time and a place for everything. We see the importance of balance also in the gospels, where we see Jesus finding a strong balance between prayer off to Himself and action with and around other people.

Jesus had such a powerful earthly ministry because He knew that, even as 100 percent deity, His 100 percent humanity required He take the proper time for rest and rejuvenation so He could have the physical human strength necessary to affect superhuman change.

Jesus' biggest bone of contention with the Pharisees was that they lived unbalanced lives. They followed the letter of each one of the laws of Moses, but they could not (or would not) show love toward others, thereby proving themselves unwilling to balance their mastery of the law with a lifestyle that could affect kingdom building.

In the same way, it is necessary to take steps to balance ourselves out so we can maintain the mental and physical stamina necessary for a life and ministry of longevity. It might be a hermeneutical stretch to connect these scriptures to the role of hobbies in our lives, but the importance of having hobbies is undeniable. Like the Pharisees, do people only know you by your position? Do you have an identity beyond the collar, beyond the robe, beyond the title?

Are you struggling to rediscover the essence of who you are, now that you have stepped away from the pastorate? One thing that will help you tremendously in this process of rediscovery is becoming reacquainted with hobbies, with things you like to do outside of ministry, with low-stress, non-spiritual (but wholesome) activities that allow you to not take yourself so seriously.

Our calling is such an integral part of who we are as complete human beings, but it's not the only part. Discovering or rediscovering who you are in addition to that calling is a vital piece to the process of rebuilding your foundation and restoring your life to a place of usefulness and vitality in the kingdom. Burnout and resignation may have brought you to a place where no one calls you "Pastor" or "Reverend" anymore, but once you've introduced some balance to your life, what people call you begins to matter less and less, and how God knows you takes precedence. The sooner you realize you're so much more than your position, the better your rebuilding process will be, for you'll begin to love yourself again, whether you have the position or not.

PRACTICAL APPLICATION

"Hey, Marc, man...you gonna play fantasy football this season? C'mon man, join my league. It's gonna be fun!"

The year was 2010, and I was entering my third year of pastoring, following our Annual Conference that August. One of my best friends had been asking me to join his league for three seasons and wasn't giving up. I had politely turned him down the two years previous because I was busy.

All my life, I've been busy. Busy with this pile of homework. Busy with this project. Busy with extracurricular classes. Busy all the way through undergrad. Busy with seminary.

Busy allowing my ever-heightened sense of responsibility and my strict task orientation to convince me I needed to skip social activities, skip recreation, skip having fun to get things done.

This time, though, I had just enough margin in my life. There's never been a time in my life when I wasn't swamped with responsibility, and August 2010 was no exception, but this time around, I figured I'd have just enough time to make it happen.

Little did I know, my wife and I would find out a few weeks later that we were expecting our first child. With the rigors and fears of a challenging pregnancy, all that margin I thought I had went flying out of the window. But I was determined to make fantasy football work this time.

So began my journey toward falling in love with what has become my favorite hobby. Not only has fantasy football completely captured my attention, quenching my thirst for competition and facilitating my creativity in assembling the best group of 15 players I can find, but fantasy football has become much more than a game to me. It's been a lifeline.

During some of my darkest days of pastoral ministry, being able to whip out my smartphone, open up my fantasy football app, and scour the waiver wire for rejected, overlooked, or emerging talent to help improve my team excited me, lifted my broken spirits from the doldrums of despair, and took away the sting of disappointment, even if only for a moment.

Rekindling the love for and consistent practice of spiritual disciplines is critically important in the process of rebuilding your life from the devastation of burnout. We will cover that in detail in the next chapter.

Seeking a healthy balance, however, through aspects unrelated to ministry is just as important as any spiritual discipline or anything else specifically related to ministry in helping you gain or maintain sanity and ultimately achieve peace in your life.

A peace absolutely necessary for picking up the pieces and realizing life after burnout.

The benefits of balance

For me, this balancing process has yielded three distinct benefits, positive outcomes from my involvement with people, places, and things outside of pastoral ministry that have given me a healthier perspective of life in ministry.

1. People – Building or maintaining relationships with people outside of my ministry context has helped me remember who I am beyond my position, without my title.

In chapter 5, I talked about how I had very few people I could talk to in ministry while I was enduring my burnout experience. Saying that, though, without qualification, understates the impact the people I did talk to on a regular basis had on my life during this most arduous season. Having gone through what I've suffered, I appreciate them now more than ever.

Thanks to the GroupMe app, one of a handful of smartphone apps I use every single day, I am able to talk daily to four of my closest friends, fine gentlemen I've known most of my life and whom I consider brothers.

Each of us lives in different states and a couple, even different time zones, but through this platform, we are able to communicate regularly, as if we're still teenagers, sitting at a Denny's or Coney Island for a late-night meal and epic conversation [1].

Because we've all been so close for so long, we are able to drop the pretension, talk openly, and "keep it 100" with one another. Over the past several years of adulthood, we've been there for one another through births, deaths, job losses, career changes, moments of doubt and trepidation, health challenges and triumphs, and new ventures.

Through every win, we've celebrated with one another like it was our own accomplishment. Through every loss, we've consoled each other like it was our own personal defeat.

I certainly experienced this friendship on the latter side of the spectrum during my final year of pastoral ministry. When I had leaders who turned their backs on me, when I had people who criticized me for being too transparent in sharing my struggles on social media (when in all actuality, I actually shared just a very small portion of what I was going through at the time), when I was around some well-meaning colleagues who couldn't hear my cries for help because they had their own struggles to deal with, my biggest source of encouragement, other than my wife, was my band of brothers on GroupMe.

I shared almost everything with them. Whatever they did not know, only my wife knew. Every time someone said something crazy to me, I shared it with them. Every time a member or officer did something underhanded, I talked to them about it. Whenever someone I trusted in ministry questioned my loyalty, my integrity, or my work ethic, I told my closest friends about it.

And through it all, never once did they judge or question me. They always had my back.

Here's the thing, though. These brothers are laymen. They aren't biblical scholars, seminarians, or great theologians, and it's not likely that I'm ever going to sit up with these guys and break bread over such heady topics like the virtues of expository preaching, existentialism, reformed theology, apologetics, or proof of authorship of the book of Isaiah or the Pauline Epistles.

But in their being who they are, they've been exactly what I've needed in life. They knew me before the Reverend, before the lofty title, before the Doctorate. They knew me before I became somebody, back when I didn't have a lot of friends. Back when I was too shy and not confident enough about my physical appearance to ask a girl to my senior prom.

Yet, as each of us does with one another, my boys spend far more time affirming who I am now and who I aspire to be rather than who I used to be. And we all need that. We all need people in our lives who know us beyond our vocation and thereby allow us to be the absolute most authentic version of ourselves, both during our triumphs and our slip-ups.

Being able to draw encouragement from people in our lives who call us by what some like to say our "government name", instead of Pastor, Reverend, or Doctor is not just essential for facilitating the kind of balance we need to have a thriving ministry, but it's an even more important factor in the recovery and rebuilding process from pastoral burnout because in both cases, such people help us maintain a balanced view of ourselves and not allow us to get so caught up in our position that we forget how to live our lives without it.

Furthermore, having close, reliable friends outside of your professional context is especially important for us men and women of the cloth because society expects us to be "always on" and never have moments of weakness, in public or in private. Close friends who are not in ministry assist us greatly in remaining sane, even when our ministries are under attack, because they don't pressure us to be perfect.

I cannot possibly understate how important it is to have at least one or two people in your corner who allow you to be you and who don't pressure you to be perfect all the time. Your burnout recovery or prevention absolutely depends on it.

2. Places – *Stepping outside my ministry context and spending some time outside of the local church helped me make observations or discoveries completely unrelated to ministry that actually gave me a new perspective on ministry.*

Before I experienced burnout and resigned from pastoral ministry, I can count on one hand the number of Sundays I was not at a corporate worship service of some kind, somewhere.

After nearly 32 years of consistent church attendance as a young person, a lay member, a minister in training, an associate minister, and eventually, a pastor, I suddenly found myself without a pulpit, without a church home, and without a preaching engagement. It was a brand new, completely different feeling.

My wife and I did find a temporary home with a ministry that has done nothing but show us love since the moment we arrived, but we are not members there, and while we are regular attendees, we are not there every Sunday. Also, I assist my mother-in-law with her ministry, but she meets once a month, either on a Saturday or Sunday, depending on scheduling. I actually really enjoy Saturday worship, but it opens up my Sundays, and honestly, I am not at all used to it.

Not so long ago, I stood tall atop the ivory tower of vocational ministry with my advanced degree, my lofty position, my accomplishments, and all the unintentional pretentiousness that came with those badges of honor.

In that former life, when I would go to the restaurant or the grocery store or run any other errand Sunday afternoon after worship, I would look around at people in plain clothes and think in my mind about how depraved they were because they hadn't been to church that day. I used to think the same thing looking at my casually dressed neighbors as I left my subdivision for worship every Sunday morning.

I had a completely myopic view of the Christian walk that said that while Sunday church attendance wasn't the be-all, end-all of one's faith, not attending anywhere was certainly a negative indicator of one's relationship with Christ.

If you love Jesus, you need to be in his house on a Sunday, period. Or so I thought.

That is, until I found myself working on projects or running some errands on a few Sunday mornings and firing up the web browser on my phone or iPad to catch the stream of a sermon at one of two or three churches I keep up with on a regular basis.

I had become the person I used to question.

One Sunday morning around 10am, on my way to Kroger, as I was taking the back way out of my subdivision, I made a realization. When I got to Kroger, that realization only solidified.

Driving through the neighborhood, I looked to my left and to my right to observe people taking out their lawnmowers to begin working on their yards. Once I arrived at the grocery store, I saw a number of casually dressed individuals casually strolling through the store doing their grocery shopping.

These shoppers, just like my neighbors I had passed to get to the store, were in no real hurry to complete their tasks. They had no urgency because it appeared they had all day to do whatever they needed to do. Sunday, for them and for a majority of Americans, is a day of rest, recreation, and recalibration for the week ahead. And neither of those three Rs includes the Lord.

Now, it's possible that some of the people I was observing either worshipped on Saturday or would be attending a service Sunday evening, both of which I've found myself doing in this season in my life. It was wrong of me to assume people weren't churchgoers because they weren't in worship at 11am.

The bigger realization was with these three Rs. When people are spending their Sundays, possibly the only free or not completely booked day of their week, comfortably *resting*, engaging in *recreational activities*, or *recalibrating* themselves for the upcoming work week, you can imagine it's probably very difficult to convince them of the necessity of following a Christ Who desires you to surrender your Sundays and focus on worshipping Him.

As Christians, we're fooling ourselves if we think we're going to win new converts to the faith and disciple those converts into a life that glorifies Christ with the local church in its current state of disarray.

We can't expect people to give up their comfortable Sundays to passionately pursue Christ within the context and confines of the institutional church if pastors and laypeople are always fighting; if the church rumor mill churns publicly from house to house, throughout the community, from Sunday afternoon until the following Sunday morning; if churches can't give an honest, accurate account of their finances; if men and women of God who preach the gospel are living with no more humility, moral clarity, or sexual responsibility than those who've never heard the gospel.

After 32 years, I finally got to experience how the majority spends its Sundays, and I must say, it was very relaxing and refreshing. We who are saved, we who spend Sunday after Sunday in the house of God have a LOT of work to do.

It took being away from the local church for a while to gain this perspective.

When you're sick, it's regularly considered a wise practice to stay away from the people, things, and, in this case, the places that caused the sickness, if, in fact, we know what those things are.

In the same way, if you know your involvement in the local church precipitated burnout in your life, it would be hasty and unwise to expect to be able to jump right back into another local church just because it's the right thing to do. It's okay to step away for a little while if you know you need to, if you know your life, your sanity depends on it.

You're not a bad Christian if you need to worship at Bedside Baptist for a season. Don't worry, you're still saved.

3. Things — Seeking new hobbies or rekindling my love for old ones provided me much-needed sources of encouragement and put me in the mode of continuous discovery and continuous improvement.

I've already touched on a few sources that have helped me keep some semblance of a balance—fantasy football and GroupMe. I can't tell you how vital these diversions were in keeping me afloat during my darkest moments.

During my year of ministry hell, as I've commonly referred to it, I had a stellar fantasy football season and came in second place in my league, only a few points and a few shaky decisions away from the championship. A year later, mere months removed from my pastorate, I won the league championship, with ten straight victories to end the season, many of which came in dramatic fashion. Many people in the league said my team, *Pastor's Power Players*, was charmed or especially blessed by God that year. I'll take it.

Recreational activities like fantasy football that have nothing to do with ministry allow me to relax and bring some balance to my ministry. Another such hobby I've picked up over the last few years is podcasting.

A podcast is an online broadcast that offers on-demand, episodic programming in the form of audio or video files that can be downloaded onto one's computer, smartphone, or other mobile device.

In the introduction, I reflected briefly on how podcasting essentially saved my ministry. I started listening to podcasts the last three months of my short tenure at my previous church, and while I still ended up burning out and leaving my previous charge, I left with a much better mindset than I would have otherwise.

I might have completely left ministry, if not for the encouragement I received from listening to hours upon hours of programming from men and women just like me who are striving for excellence and seeking to do something positive in the world with the gifts God has given them (whether they know it was God who gave them or not).

In June 2013, I started off with one podcast and spent

weeks listening at 1x speed to most of its episodes on my hour-long commute to and from the office.

As of the publishing of this book, I have an extensive library of 72 podcasts I listen to on a daily or weekly basis at 2x speed. There are very few moments in my day when I'm not listening to something, and for the most part, it's not music, but podcasts that dominate my ear.

What made me fall in love with the medium of podcasting is that podcast hosts and producers are largely entrepreneurial, either by profession or at least in mindset, which is necessary to build a sizable and engaged audience for an independent Internet radio show that doesn't have the financial backing of local or nationally syndicated terrestrial radio programs and networks.

Because the large majority of people who host or produce podcasts are entrepreneurs, they look at the world much differently than how most people do, so what these people teach on their shows constantly challenges the status quo and, even more so, challenges your thinking.

Some of the podcasts I listen to are ministry-related, and those are a blessing, but most of them are of the business or documentary/NPR-style genre. Some of the hosts are believers, but many of them aren't. But regardless of belief system, I've been able to learn a lot and grow from every show I listen to. In the past two years of podcast listening, I have been able to expose myself to so many new ideas that have significantly challenged and expanded me as a minister of the gospel, an entrepreneur, a husband and father, and as an overall person. Podcasting has even helped me be more consistent with my daily scripture readings.

Constantly exposing myself to new things not altogether related to ministry has not only helped me become a more well-read, more informed, better person, but it's helped take the pressure off of myself in my recovery and rebuilding process because I've been able to give my mind a break from the struggles I've endured and my somewhat uncertain (but otherwise bright) future.

Considering the impact people, places, and things have on your life beyond ministry is key in helping you find the balance you need to recover from burnout and/or avoid it in the future. Taking these steps has helped me tremendously in my rebuilding process.

After you've preached the sermon, said Amen, taken off the collar and the robe, and gone back home, you still need to live. Pursuing a balanced life will help you emerge victoriously from your struggles to live abundantly and authentically, in a way that glorifies God and builds God's kingdom.

Who we are and what we do are closely intertwined, but they are not one in the same. The sooner we understand that, the better off we'll be.

DEVOTIONAL POINTS
Reflect
1. Think about the things you like to do that have no spiritual connotation whatsoever. How often do you do those activities? Start doing those things more, and stop short of them being an obsession.

2. Consider the opportunity God may give you to minister in the midst of whatever your hobby is, if it involves other people. This ministry is something you'll never have to force, but just keep it in the back of your mind because you never know. You may not be pastoring right now, you may never again pastor in the local church, but you have a ministry that yet lives inside of you, and God may use that ministry in unimaginable ways.

Read
1. Matthew 23, Ecclesiastes 3:1-8.

Pray
#PrayForYourPastor

Your pastor needs your prayers concerning recreational activities. Does the atmosphere within your church and the congregational expectations placed on your pastor provide opportunity for him or her to discover or engage in hobbies? If not, pray those things happen because your pastor absolutely needs balance in his or her life, for with more balance, your pastor will be the very best he or she can be.

Pray for your church to be more open-minded about incorporating recreation and entertainment into the life of the ministry, and pray that your pastor will be empowered to take the lead in that initiative. Pray that neither you nor your pastor take yourselves so seriously that you forget how to laugh, how to play, how to have a good time. Pray for your pastor to be a well-balanced, spiritually healthy individual, and pray for the church to be the same, for such will help you be most effective in kingdom building.

My prayer for you...

Father God, in Jesus' name, speak to your fallen servants. Encourage them right now in your word, and let them know they are still worthwhile, valuable people with a lot to offer the body of Christ, with or without their title or position. Let your recovering pastors who are looking to one day reenter full-time ministry know, Lord, that it is perfectly acceptable to take some time throughout each week to engage in wholesome activities that have nothing to do with preaching, teaching, visiting, or counseling.

Let those of your servants who are still looking for direction for the future or who have no desire to be a pastor ever again take this time in their rebuilding process to learn about themselves and truly discern who they are outside the pulpit so they can be happy and hopeful about their future, whatever it looks like and wherever you may take them. Minister to your servants powerfully in the midst of whatever hobbies or activities they engage in, and afford them to minister to others organically within those hobbies or activities. Give your servants balance as they rebuild, and empower them to live balanced lives moving forward, in Jesus' name, Amen.

Balance

III
REBUILD YOUR FAITH

Once the recovering pastor has reached a place of mental stability and has reconnected with the essence of who he or she is outside the pulpit, it is then necessary to rebuild his or her faith. At this point in the rebuilding process, the pastor must rekindle his or her love for and faith in Christ. As the man or woman of God takes the necessary steps here, he or she will be better able to answer the following questions: *What makes you who you are in Christ? What or who motivates you to do ministry?* As the recovering pastor's faith is rebuilt, resolve is strengthened, maturity is increased, and his or her mindset regarding what he or she has been through can begin to change.

-7-
REDISCOVERY
Back to basics

"But I have this against you, that you have abandoned the love you had at first. Remember then from what you have fallen; repent, and do the works you did at first."
Revelation 2:4-5a

THEOLOGICAL REFLECTION

The church as Ephesus was the first of seven churches that were to receive a prophetic letter of warning, instruction, and encouragement, according to the revelation of Jesus Christ to the apostle John. In the letter, Jesus had only one issue with the Ephesians—They had "abandoned the love [they] had at first." They were patient, enduring, and strong in the faith, but they had gotten away from the love they had when they first began their journey. And we know from the words of Christ that the Ephesians had fallen away from this first love because they were no longer doing the works they had done at first. In other words, they were no longer practicing the spiritual disciplines they had adopted when they first became believers. They had stopped doing the things they used to do when they knew less about God, when they didn't have their positions, when they were babes in Christ and didn't have any spiritual authority.

Just an aside, we must always caution ourselves against holding an unbalanced view of the role of God's grace in our lives, overemphasizing grace and prioritizing it over the pursuit of holy and righteous living. It's certainly true that we are not saved by our own merit, and grace is the only thing that keeps us from being separated from God, but just like oil changes, transmission flushes, and tire rotations keep a vehicle in tip-top operating condition, our works, our habits, our daily lifestyle decisions, the things we must do to uphold a holy standard are important for maintaining a life pleasing to God.

Yes, God's grace makes all the difference, but if we're not doing things on a daily basis to actively reflect that grace, we're wasting it and leaving ourselves dangerously susceptible to falling away from God. Some well-intentioned believers will proudly purport, "All you have to do is believe and the spirit of Christ will transform you." To that, I say not exactly. We have a prominent role to play in our own salvation. We don't fulfill that role in our own strength, yet the responsibility is still ours to show up and do the work and lean on God for the increase.

Each of us is mandated to "work out our own salvation with fear and trembling," as Paul admonished the Philippians (2:12). This is the same Paul who, in his letters to Rome and Galatia, constantly taught against strict adherence to the law of Moses as a means to salvation and argued for the grace of God alone making us righteous before God. He says as much to the Romans (6:15-23):

> *What then? Should we sin because we are not under law but under grace? By no means! Do you not know that if you present yourselves to anyone as obedient slaves, you are slaves of the one whom you obey, either of sin, which leads to death, or of obedience, which leads to righteousness? But thanks be to God that you, having once been slaves of sin, have become obedient from the heart to the form of teaching to which you were entrusted, and that you, having been set free from sin, have become slaves of righteousness. I am speaking in human terms because of your natural limitations. For just as you once presented your members as slaves to impurity and to greater and greater iniquity, so now present*

your members as slaves to righteousness for sanctification.

When you were slaves of sin, you were free in regard to righteousness. So what advantage did you then get from the things of which you now are ashamed? The end of those things is death. But now that you have been freed from sin and enslaved to God, the advantage you get is sanctification. The end is eternal life. For the wages of sin is death, but the free gift of God is eternal life in Christ Jesus our Lord.

So Paul was teaching the Romans that grace does not nullify our mandate to live righteously, but rather it ensures our ability to do so, through a strength not our own but God's. While we no longer live under the law, we still must put the work in daily to become the people God has called us to be.

Back to the Ephesians, Jesus lets them know unequivocally that they have some work to do. In Revelation 2:5, Jesus tells them clearly, "Remember then from what you have fallen; repent and do the works you did at first." What are the first works? These first works speak to the regular practice of spiritual disciplines—prayer, fasting, study of God's word, regular fellowship with other believers, and others—that keep our hearts, our minds, and, most importantly, our spirits in line and in focus on Christ.

Much like balanced eating ensures we have the proper blend of vitamins and nutrients that allow our bodies to operate at optimal condition, no matter how rigorous our schedule, spiritual disciplines give our spirits what we need to live optimally and victoriously, even in seasons of our most intense struggle. We're doing a great work for the kingdom, the greatest work we can do for God. We have been and inevitably will continue to be attacked by Satan because of who we are and what we do. We must be spiritually alive and ready to withstand these attacks to avoid breaking down and burning out in the future.

PRACTICAL APPLICATION

On a Friday afternoon, I got the call from my Bishop, informing me of the church to where I would be appointed and transferred. That evening, I had two difficult phone conversations, one with my faithful Assistant Pastor and the other, with my head trustee and the Mr. Do-It-All at the church (every church has one), informing them of the Bishop's decision and asking them to pass the message to as many members as possible and make sure they come to church Sunday for what would be my last service there as their pastor.

That last service was an abbreviated one because I wanted to take the time to say goodbye to my members before driving back across the border to Detroit, where the closing service for the Michigan Annual Conference was being held, so I could receive the certificate of appointment to my new church.

Monday morning following the appointment, I called the church office but did not get an answer. My wife and I later drove up to the church to take a look at the area and hopefully talk to someone, but no one was there. I would later learn the church administrative office was open Tuesday through Thursday. My intention was to have a meet-and-greet time of fellowship with the people and take time to meet with the ministerial staff to cover the church in prayer before my first service.

None of this happened, however, because my wife was admitted to the hospital immediately after her appointment Tuesday morning. Jada's due date wasn't for another month, yet we really didn't have a good idea when she was coming. My wife's doctor had already informed us that, as with Candace, Jada would not stay in the oven the full 40 weeks.

It was now week 36, so we had to be prepared for her to come at any time. It was still a shock, though, to have to drive my wife straight from her appointment to the hospital, where she would give birth to my youngest daughter that night.

About an hour after my wife was admitted, I received a

call from the Steward Board Pro-Tem, welcoming me to the church and letting me know he'd be my point person in coordinating a smooth transition. I thanked him for calling and told him where I was and what was going on at that moment. I also let him know it was my intention to schedule a time that week to meet at least some of the people and pray.

Well, life happened, and none of what I intended took place. There was just too much going on, and I was just not able to make it all work for everybody. I could not have that meet-and-greet, and, unlike with my first church, I was unable to make that prayer meeting happen.

At my first church, we saturated the entire facility in prayer. God met us there that evening, and God blessed my ministry there. At this new church, I was not able to have that same time of prayer. Did that make a difference in how things turned out at this church? Would things have worked out differently had I been able to pray over the building, as I had desired?

These are questions I cannot answer, unfortunately. What I do know for sure and have known for many years, however, is the power of prayer. I can say with a great deal of certainty that I've never done anything right in my life without prayer, and all I've done wrong in my life, I did because I tried to lean on my own wisdom, rather than petitioning God for God's wisdom in the situation.

The context of prayer is also important to consider. By the time I had burned out at this new church, I was at the point that when I arrived at the office everyday, I started out my day with prayer in the sanctuary, but those prayers were simply for me to have a positive attitude and get through the day without losing my mind. Honestly, through the fault of no one else but me, I had allowed the hustle and bustle of daily life in pastoral ministry to take me away from a consistent prayer life. By the time I had resumed praying fervently on a daily basis, my mind and spirit were already too far gone for it to make a difference.

The importance of spiritual disciplines

Prayer is but one of a number of spiritual disciplines, or consistent acts we perform that place our spirits in alignment with God and God's will for our lives, thereby enabling us to suppress our carnality, affirm our spirituality, and be the most godly version of ourselves on a consistent basis.

Richard Foster, author of *Celebration of Discipline*, doesn't explicitly define either the term "spiritual disciplines" or "disciplines", but he does speak to their purpose and importance on pages 1 and 2 of his book, where he states, "Superficiality is the curse of our age," and that "The classical Disciplines of the spiritual life call us to move beyond surface living into the depths. They invite us to explore the inner caverns of the spiritual realm." He goes on to say, "The purpose of the Disciplines is liberation from the stifling slavery to self-interest and fear."

On page 2, Foster offers the following wisdom about the accessibility of spiritual disciplines for all human beings, regardless of Christian experience or theological background:

> *We must not be led to believe that the Disciplines are only for spiritual giants and hence beyond our reach, or only for contemplatives who devote all their time to prayer and meditation. Far from it. God intends the Disciplines of the spiritual life to be for ordinary human beings...We need not be well advanced in matters of theology to practise the Disciplines. Recent converts...can and should practise them. The primary requirement is a longing after God.*

Spiritual disciplines are rarely the topic of conversation in Christian preaching and teaching, news, commentaries, debates, or literature, but their centrality in the well-balanced, well-lived life of the believer is undeniable.

Why are spiritual disciplines vital to burnout recovery?

When you've experienced burnout in pastoral ministry, you've experienced, I believe, the worst kind of personal or professional failure, in terms of public perception and expectation, no matter how realistic or unrealistic.

In his book, *Why Pastors Quit*, Bo Lane, founder of ExPastors.com, a fantastic resource for former pastors, pastors in transition, or burnt-out pastors on temporary leave, illustrates beautifully the internal struggle a former pastor faces when reconciling his/her decision to leave pastoral ministry [1]:

> *I'm an expastor. It's kind of awkward saying that, to be honest. Almost as though it's sinful. Like, "I used to be a good person, but now that I've left serving the church in a full-time capacity, I've spun into this dark element of evil doingness." But I've thought about it quite a bit and still don't know what else you'd call someone who was once a pastor, other than an expastor...it's awkward. And not only is it awkward saying it, it's just as awkward living it out. As an individual who served many years as a pastor in full-time ministry, I find it difficult at times to find my place in this world. And I'm sure many others who have also left the ministry feel the same way I do...How does the church process someone like me?*

It's one thing to leave a corporate job because of burnout, disillusionment, disagreement with the company's business practices, or simply to strike out on your own and start your own business, but it's another thing entirely to actually leave ministry because of any one of the above reasons, especially burnout or disillusionment.

You're not supposed leave ministry.

If you're preaching the gospel of Jesus Christ, if you're a servant of the Most High God, if you're a man or woman of the cloth, how could you possibly experience burnout? Don't you serve the Almighty, everlasting, omnipresent, omnipotent God? Shouldn't God's power have kept you from burning out? Didn't God call you? Where's your faith?

Your decision will damage your witness for Christ.

I've interacted with Bo quite a bit online, but I do not know him personally, nor have I asked him for any kind of deeper insight on this passage. I can imagine, however, that these must have been some of the questions and comments he wrestled with either internally or externally when he left pastoral ministry. These certainly were all thoughts I dealt with when I made my departure.

It is because of the struggle to answer these questions and quell the negativity of vocal and non-vocal naysayers that the burnt-out pastor can be in such a malaise after stepping down.

Recovering from such discouragement and regaining or maintaining faith in God and, more difficult but more importantly, in God's people requires the former pastor to return to the basics of his or her faith. This recovery calls for the man or woman of God to rebuild his/her spirituality through the rediscovery of spiritual disciplines.

The recovering pastor must embrace or re-embrace the basics of holy living and, as Jesus, through the Apostle John, admonished the church at Ephesus in Revelation 2:1-7, return to his/her first love.

We return to our first love by muting the noise—the criticisms, the voices, the snide remarks, the bashing, the negativity, the insecurities, the uncertainties about the future—and rediscover the love of Jesus Christ through the consistent of spiritual disciplines.

The disciplines

Contrary to the beliefs of some financially influential laypeople and of denominational officials who had the power to affect my position in ministry, I never, ever neglected my pastoral responsibilities. I consistently prepared myself, to the best of my abilities, to do the work of ministry. I practiced spiritual disciplines.

But many months after my resignation, I realized what I had done was insufficient. I needed a refresher course in the practice of spiritual disciplines. And I knew exactly the source I needed to consult.

In the African Methodist Episcopal Church, the process from Licentiate (Minister in Training) to ordained Elder lasts a minimum of four years, depending on your level of educational attainment and which track you declare (Local or

Itinerant) when you enter the Board of Examiners ministers' training program.

The instructor for my Second-Year Studies class in the Board of Examiners assigned us the aforementioned classic work, *Celebration of Discipline*, by Richard Foster. Of all the books I was assigned during my years of ministry training, Foster's work was among the most influential to my ministry, so much so that when I got to the point of my rebuilding process that I knew I needed to revisit spiritual disciplines and the fundamentals of holy living, this was the book I thought of instantly.

Foster outlines 12 disciplines—four inward, four outward, and four corporate—that we must learn, embrace, and consistently practice for a deeper spiritual experience with God:

Inward: Meditation, Prayer, Fasting, Study

Outward: Simplicity, Solitude, Submission, Service

Corporate: Confession, Worship, Guidance, Celebration

I won't describe these disciplines here and regurgitate the entire book, as it's his material and not mine. You owe it to yourself to purchase this work and read it for yourself. Pick it up, and let it bless you.

Moment of transparency: My knowing I needed to grab Celebration off the bookshelf and dust it off doesn't mean I instantly began re-devouring it. It was actually in the process of writing this book that I began revisiting Foster. And the whole time, I've been asking myself why I didn't go straight to my bookshelf when I had the inkling to grab the book. I was delaying my own spirit's delight. Again, I write this book not as an expert, but as a sojourner on the road to recovery, a partner in the process of rebuilding from burnout. I therefore have a long way to go in many of these areas of consecration, especially with fasting and taking care of my physical body. The rebuilding process is ongoing.

As we strive to put our lives back together again, rediscover who we are as individuals, and reconnect with the vision God has placed within each of us, I invite you to rediscover and recommit to the power and practice of spiritual disciplines and let the anointing therein repair the broken places in your life. As you rekindle "the love you had at first" for Christ through these practical applications of Christian spirituality, God can begin to renew your vitality and possibly even your passion for ministry. In the process of rebuilding your faith, the rediscovery of spiritual disciplines is a necessary step.

DEVOTIONAL POINTS

Reflect

1. Recall how you felt when you first accepted Christ into your life and began living accordingly. What specific actions did you take, or what spiritual disciplines did you practice that were consistent with your confession of Christ? Even if you look back on those times with the belief that you had a little too much zeal, can you honestly find some room to re-incorporate some of those basic practices into your life today as a more mature Christian?

2. Think back to when you first accepted your call to preach the gospel. Do you study and meditate on the word of God more or less now than you did back then?

3. Which area of consecration do you find most challenging? Could an accountability partner help you grow in that area?

Read

1. Revelation 2:1-8

2. *Celebration of Discipline* by Richard Foster, for all the reasons discussed above.

3. Blog post, "Ten Joy Stealers in Ministry (And How to Get It Back)," by Thom Rainer, pastoral leadership blogger and President and CEO of Lifeway Christian Resources [2]. This blog post about the various aspects of local church ministry that cause a pastor to lose his or her joy is relevant here from the standpoint of being able to look at these and see where a rediscovery of spiritual disciplines could address

them. Dr. Rainer lists 10 joy stealers and offers solutions for each, but several of them could be also addressed with consistent and fervent practice of spiritual disciplines. Read this post and see if you can identify them.

Pray
#PrayForYourPastor
Your pastor is bombarded with responsibilities, distractions, meetings, conflicts, and other challenges on a weekly basis, inside and outside of the church, that have the potential to limit study and consecration time if he or she is not careful. Properly meeting the multifaceted demands of ministry while remaining faithful to the basics of personal and professional preparation requires your pastor to be a time management wizard. Your pastor cannot waste a single minute in the day and still be effective, so your help and your prayers are desperately needed. Pray that your pastor has the energy necessary to fulfill all of his or her duties effectively, giving proper time to each task.

Pray for God to grant your pastor the mental and spiritual wherewithal to exercise sound stewardship over his or her day and the courage to say no to those things that are not in the best interest of his or her time. Pray that your pastor can give proper attention to every responsibility and still have time to consecrate him/herself through faithfulness to spiritual disciplines. Pray for God to show you and your fellow church members how you can best assist your pastor and not be a distraction to him or her in any way. Pray not only for ways to not be a distraction to your pastor, but even more so for opportunities to help your pastor accomplish more each day and maximize his or her personal preparation time, thereby being as effective a pastor as possible.

My prayer for you...
God, my prayer for recovering, rebuilding pastors here is for the anointing to rediscover what really matters. When your servants were pastoring, they were hit with personal and

professional challenges from every side, and they let their personal time with you wane. Your recovering pastors allowed their faithfulness to spiritual disciplines to fade, and their connection with you began to slip.

Rekindle within your servants a deep love for the basics of a personal relationship with you—prayer, fasting, study of your word, worship, service, and others. In this process of rediscovery, I pray you touch your servants so tangibly, so deeply that the joy they feel is almost as if they are experiencing these disciplines for the first time. May this experience of rediscovery boost their confidence and brighten their outlook as they embark on the rest of this rebuilding journey. In Jesus' name, Amen.

-8-
LESSONS
What would you do differently?
"My child, do not despise the Lord's discipline
or be weary of his reproof,
for the Lord reproves the one he loves,
as a father the son in whom he delights."
Proverbs 3:11-12

THEOLOGICAL REFLECTION

I will stop just short of saying that this text and others like it are self-explanatory, but the concept being described here is universal. There are 49 occurrences of the word "fool" in Proverbs and 21 of the plural "fools", and many of them condemn the inability to accept correction or learn from mistakes as foolish behavior that lacks wisdom. The wise person is not the one who avoids mistakes, but rather is the one who learns from the mistakes he or she makes. A survey of scripture will reveal that those figures in scripture who took advantage of their mistakes as opportunities to learn and grow were blessed by God, and those who did not were cursed by their stubbornness.

Examining the conflict between brothers Cain and Abel (Genesis 4:1-16), God clearly told Cain that he had no reason to be jealous about God's accepting Abel's offering over his and that he had the opportunity to rectify that and give God the proper offering, but Cain ignored God's words and killed his brother. Cain didn't learn his lesson.

A significant portion of the Pentateuch covered a wilderness period from Egyptian captivity to the Promised Land that, from purely a distance standpoint, shouldn't have lasted more than a few months, but instead lasted 40 years and cost everyone's life except Joshua and Caleb. Why? Because the Israelites didn't learn from their mistakes and kept repeating them, perpetuating a seemingly never-ending cycle of sin, punishment, petition, forgiveness, righteous living, spiritual cockiness, and sin again between God and God's chosen people. The Israelites didn't learn their lesson and suffered for it over and over again for a generation.

King David was a wise man who let his way with the ladies get the best of him for a season and ended up doing a number of things he was not supposed to be doing, all of which resulted in some unfortunate consequences for him (2 Samuel 11-12). In the end, though, he did actually learn from his mistakes and enjoyed a wildly successful kingship from that season on. More about David in the next chapter.

Jonah was not so wise, though. He understood the sole reason for his being in the belly of a whale was that he tried to run in the opposite direction of where God had called him to go. He didn't have enough good sense, however, to reflect back on his mistakes and appreciate God's forgiveness in his life, instead of being upset about God's forgiving people he didn't like. Jonah didn't learn his lesson.

And as will be discussed later, two of the original twelve disciples each betrayed Christ in his own way, yet because only one learned his lesson from his betrayal, we only remember one as a betrayer, while the other is known as the rock upon which the church of Jesus Christ was built. One has namesakes in human beings and churches all over the world, throughout every generation, and the other, yeah, not so much.

The recovering, rebuilding pastor, by this point, has already dealt with the oppressive feelings of blame and shame, has asked him/herself "What if?", and has wondered countless times what could have been. I know I have. What we're talking about here, though, is much different. There are many factors, both internal and external, that lead to burnout and resignation. Immediately at that point of burnout, the resigning pastor is definitely dealing with a number of strong emotions that won't allow him or her to have any kind of genuine, level-headed perspective about what they've been through.

Perspective—the kind of perspective needed to thoughtfully consider lessons learned—comes only after considerable inner work has been done, and that only comes with time. How much time? No one can honestly answer that for sure, but however long that inner work of healing and restoration takes, it absolutely must happen so the recovering pastor can be in the frame of mind necessary to identify the lessons learned from his or her burnout experience.

As free-willed but flawed human beings, we go through seasons of intense trial, and we certainly make plenty of mistakes of head and heart along the way. But as Christians, we can experience repentance, forgiveness, healing, and restoration in Christ Jesus, regardless of what we've been through. Perhaps we didn't leave the pastorate because of a decline into moral failure. Maybe we never took a dime from the treasury while we were in charge. Maybe our record of leadership was spotless and completely above reproach, and our integrity could not be questioned at any point. You may not have a single skeleton in your closet.

All of this may be true, but along the way, something happened that you are not proud of and that you could have done differently. Please take advantage of the opportunity you have in this rebuilding process to consider lessons learned and grow from the situation, lest your season of trial be wasted, as with Jonah.

PRACTICAL APPLICATION

I defended my Doctor of Ministry dissertation on a cold, (lightly) snowy Thursday November afternoon at Ecumenical

Theological Seminary in Detroit, Michigan to a committee of four individuals and an audience of five more: the admissions director, the academic dean, a member of the Board of Directors, one colleague (and another who had to leave early) and my beautiful wife. The size of this group fostered an intimacy that allowed for an extremely candid and deeply personal question-and-answer period following my presentation. It was a very different Q&A than what might have occurred had there been a bigger crowd.

The first question or two pertained specifically to my project, as there were a few points I found it very difficult to elaborate on in 20 short minutes of presentation. Following those project specificities ensued a conversation between a room full of doctors and myself about how the project had changed me, what I learned in the process, where I saw God taking me in the future, and how I saw God using me as a Doctor of Ministry to build the kingdom moving forward.

Of all the questions that were asked, the one question that stuck with me, though, came from the mouth of Bob, a member of my doctoral committee:

"Having gone through all you have and learning as much as you have about pastoral burnout and dealing with conflict in ministry, what would you do differently if you had to do it all over again?"

You see, as my content specialist, Bob probably read my dissertation closer than anyone on my committee, and therefore had worked with me one-on-one long enough to know this was a good question to ask me.

Bob joined my committee in early June 2014 after I had completely blown it (unintentionally) with my previous committee member in the same position, to the point where he called me to inform me he would be stepping aside as my content specialist.

That call turned out to be the best thing that happened to me all year.

The first time Bob and I met, he let me know if this partnership was going to work, I would have to fully submit to the process and be wiling to have thick skin and accept correction. And accept correction is exactly what I did.

I took heed to every piece of critique he gave me on my work because I was serious about learning, I was serious about growing, I was serious about getting better, and he told me as much at my defense, saying I was the most receptive of all the candidates he had worked with in this capacity.

Bob pushed me in ways I didn't think I could be pushed, and because of that, I think I was able to derive much greater insights than I ever thought I could have. These insights have been key to my being able to write the way I do about my experiences today. Bob was just who I needed for my project.

My wife: My number one fan

I would never dare purport to do everything right, but I do try to be as self-aware as I possibly can, oftentimes to a fault. My wife often tells me I'm too critical of myself and am too slow to give myself credit for the things I do right.

As accomplished as my wife has been in her own life, she's my number one cheerleader. She rides hard for me.

So, when Bob asked the "What would you do differently?" question, you could just see the smoke coming out of my wife's ears, not because she was upset at Bob for asking, but because she's very defensive about me and could easily remember all of the crazy things we endured together while at my previous church.

She was trying to hold her piece, but you could hear her mumbling really softly as I struggled to come up with an acceptable answer: "You don't understand. There were just a lot of extenuating circumstances. It wasn't your typical conflict," as if to answer for me: "There wasn't too much he could have done differently. He was set up from day one."

And she was right. I was indeed put into a bad situation that I couldn't do a whole lot about. The people were expecting someone different, and I was 10-15 years younger than any pastor who had ever served there and 20-25 years younger than any pastor who had served there successfully.

There were also a number of underlying issues between congregational factions that had been brewing at this church for years, and my propensity for telling the truth, going against the grain, and advocating for the underrepresented, misrepresented, and bullied only brought those issues front and center, causing the pot of church conflict to bubble over with tension and angst.

I was set up to fail from the moment I was appointed to the church. I was thrown into a fight I had nothing to do with and was left to my own devices to see my way out.

Therefore, whereas I'm usually able to compile a laundry list of takeaways from every situation, good or bad, I found myself truly struggling to come away with something I would have done differently during my one-year tenure.

What I should have done differently

After about a good 30-45 seconds of self-introspective pondering, I was finally able to drum up some insight. I told Bob the one thing I would have done differently is that I would have avoided defending my record and my anointing over the pulpit.

I was less than half the age of the average parishioner at this church, so people felt they could treat me like their son or grandson, rather than their pastor.

I couldn't handle the daily disrespect. I couldn't handle being called a boy. I couldn't handle officers questioning my credentials. I couldn't handle the secret meetings with my superiors. I couldn't handle the questions about my sermon preparation from people who weren't even paying attention and therefore could offer a single point from a single message I had ever preached.

I couldn't handle the attacks against my wife and my two girls.

All within my first six weeks there.

So, I defended myself by vocalizing my displeasure one Sunday before I began preaching. I should not have done this because even though the attacks against me were wrong and unwarranted, I subjected 100 percent of the people to a discussion I should have had with around 40 percent.

Sincere members who weren't involved in the foolishness I was dealing with were confused and/or became discouraged, and it took some time to smooth things over with them. As hard as it was to see past and overcome all the negativity, I should have spent more time celebrating the positive and focusing more on pouring into my coalition of supporters while praying for the naysayers.

So much to be thankful for, but couldn't see it

For the first time in my adult life, I was depressed, so much so that I could not see just how much I had to be thankful for in that ministry.

One of my college students, just 19 at the time, had spearheaded a youth outreach ice cream social that turned into one of the biggest evangelistic efforts the church had ever seen. I made her a steward, and to a man, to a woman, she was one of the most productive stewards I had on that board all year.

We had an after-school program at the church that, despite all the venom spewed its way and the lack of support it received from much of the membership, was doing wonderful things for the young people in the city.

Our cotillion program, a leadership and development program for young women in the city, members and non-members, celebrated its tenth anniversary during my tenure, and was the jewel of the city and state for the impact this work had on young women in preparing them for the next level in their lives.

A male component had been added to the program that year, the highlight of which was a shirt and tie program, wherein enough money was raised to gift every 11th grade young man in the city's public school system with a shirt and tie. We went to the various schools, presented the shirts and ties to the young men, and taught them how to tie them. The schools took our gifts to the next level by offering job interview training so these boys could both look and act the part.

The young ladies at the church were clamoring for a full-fledged liturgical dance ministry. Before we arrived, one or two of them would dance every once in a while, but not to the extent that they so desired. My wife, an experienced and accomplished dancer, took all the girls under her wing and had begun to build a ministry they could be proud of.

Many people didn't like the direction they thought the church was headed in under my leadership, so they stopped doing many of the things they had always done, hoping to stall progress and make me look bad. Other people who had never had leadership positions began to step up and provide great service to the church. One such member started to realize her call to work with young people and began serving in a mighty way in the Christian Education department. Since my departure, she has continued to grow and has become the Director of Christian Education at the church.

With time away comes perspective

Despite the negativity all around me, so much was actually going right, but I was in too much of a fog of depression to actually see it. I allowed that depression to get the best of me, and while everything I said might have been true, I lashed out in an inappropriate manner that took attention from the cross and made the preaching moment about me, rather than about Jesus. I shouldn't have done that. I'll defend my record until I'm blue in the face, but I should not have done that.

It took being away from pastoral ministry for over a year to have this kind of mindset shift. Being able to admit your shortcomings and allow God to chastise you and make you whole again comes with time, and that's why it comes at this point in the rebuilding process.

Very rarely are any of us ever 100 percent right in any situation, regardless of the circumstance. No matter how badly you've been hurt, you can always take away a lesson of self-improvement in every situation, and if you do so, you'll move one step closer to emerging victoriously from your burnout experience.

DEVOTIONAL POINTS

Reflect

1. Think about everything that went right during your pastorate. Consider your accomplishments, your triumphs, your programs that were implemented successfully under your leadership. Think about the lives that were changed while you were their pastor. Think on all these things and celebrate them.

2. Only after considering the good you did while you were a pastor should you give consideration to the lessons you can take away from your experience. But when doing so, don't just dwell on what happened to you—the lying, the intentional withholding of tithes and offerings out of spite, the scheming, the backbiting, the badmouthing of your spouse and children, whatever—because those things are easy to think about. What happened to you is always going to be top of mind. Think, rather, about your attitude, your disposition, your decision making when the chips were down. Your integrity, to this day, may be unquestioned, but at some point, you did something that could have been handled differently; you said something that could have been said with a little more tact or finesse. Nothing wrong with admitting that.

Read

1. Proverbs 3:11-12; 15:10; 18:2; Genesis 4:1-16; 2 Samuel 11-12; Jonah; the passion narratives in each of the gospel accounts.

2. Blog post, "Where There Is Smoke..." by Dale Wolery, Executive Director of the Clergy Recovery Network. (In fact, take a look at the entire site; it's a wonderful resource for burnt-out pastors.) Wolery reflects very candidly about his experiences in serving as an Associate Pastor under a Senior

Pastor who was very gifted, charismatic, and accomplished, but who had inappropriate relationships with female parishioners that went unchecked for years because of his position of prominence. Wolery writes of his lessons learned from not speaking up and holding the Senior Pastor accountable for obvious errors in judgment over the years [1].

Pray
#PrayForYourPastor

Your pastor goes through so much in ministry, some of which you see and much of which you do not see. He or she needs your prayers. It is so easy for your pastor to get bogged down with all the responsibilities of ministry and all that can happen, planned and unplanned, on a daily basis that there is little time for self-evaluation. Your pastor needs the opportunity to step away from the pulpit a few times every year to think about his or her experiences, consider the direction in which the ministry is headed, and provide an honest self-evaluation of successes and opportunities for growth.

Having this time for reflection is critical for your pastor's personal and professional development and therefore the overall health of your church. If your pastor does not have this time, pray about your church being receptive in providing it. If you're a board member and have decision-making power in this regard, pray God will move on your heart to help you and your fellow board members grant your pastor key periods of rest, recuperation, and reflection throughout the year.

My prayer for you…

Father, in the name of Jesus, I pray that as your servants have reached the point in this rebuilding process, you will help them to have the frame of mind necessary to consider lessons learned from their burnout experiences. I pray this time of introspection and self-evaluation is not a time of negativity or condemnation, but is a time when they can honestly look back at what they've been through in ministry and identify opportunities for growth and improvement.

God, I know you are not through with your servants yet, whether they reenter pastoral ministry after this season or not, and my prayer for them is that they have all the tools they need to have success in every area of their lives moving forward. And taking lessons away from previous experiences, good and bad, is key to obtaining those tools.

May this season of self-evaluation encourage your people, not depress them, and once they are encouraged, strengthen them to go share their experiences with another pastor in need. May no lesson be overlooked and no experience wasted. In Jesus' name, Amen.

Lessons

-9-
OWNERSHIP
Getting over it

"Then David rose from the ground, washed, anointed himself, and changed his clothes. He went into the house of the Lord, and worshiped; he then went to his own house; and when he asked, they set food before him and he ate."
- 2 Samuel 12:20

THEOLOGICAL REFLECTION

One of the worst pieces of advice you could ever give to someone is to tell that person, in response to their struggles with whatever they're going through, to "get over it". Now, in the word of God, we see a very clear example of what it means to get over something, and it's something we must do at some point, but it's something you absolutely cannot tell people. They must figure it out themselves. And when they do figure it out, without being callously told to do so, they take blessed ownership over their situation and live empowered lives.

David was a man after God's heart (1 Samuel 13:14; Acts 13:22). David was a wise man, a passionate worshipper, and a successful king, but when it came to the ladies, he was weak and fallible. We all have that one extra fleshly area of our lives that threatens to deter us from the plans God has for our lives if we don't stay focused and remain prayerful. For King

David, beautiful women were that gateway into his carnality. His illicit, ill-advised pursuit of Bathsheba, already a married woman illustrated just how carnal he could be in his weakest season.

In fact, it's the only time in scripture where we find David, again, a wise and faithful man, using his power for evil, instead of good. After dwelling too long in the wrong place at the wrong time and seeing the married Bathsheba naked, taking a shower, David essentially pulled strings to have Uriah, her husband, killed on the frontline of battle so he could have her to himself. God didn't honor that sin, though, as the child produced from the union of David and Bathsheba immediately following Uriah's death did not survive infancy.

With the help of some strong words from Nathan the prophet before David's young son died, the king came to understand the error of his ways and that his son would not survive because of them. Following that conversation, the child became deathly ill and after seven days, died. David had already fasted in mourning seven days by the time the child died, and if I can take a little hermeneutical license here, I'd say he was fasting as much for his role in his child's sickness as for the sickness itself. His servants were therefore very fearful to inform David when the child actually did die because they thought he'd do harm to himself.

David shocked everyone, though, by ending his fast, taking a bath, worshipping, and grabbing a bite to eat once he found out the news. David believed he had no more reason to mourn because he had already done so. He had recognized and repented for his mistakes, and he had already endured his season of mourning, so he had gotten to the place in his heart where he knew there was no point in prolonging his pain. At some point, he understood he had to pick himself up, dust himself off, and go forward in the fresh start the Lord was giving him.

We all might not approach bereavement or repentance the same way, but the truth here is universal. If you've ever burned out and walked away from something, whether it's ministry or anything else important to you, you've undoubtedly lost something, and you have a reason to mourn. And if you know there was a series of mistakes you made along the way that possibly led to that burnout, then you might be feeling even worse about yourself. At some point, though, in order to move forward with rebuilding our lives and positioning ourselves to live victoriously, we must come to a place of peace in our hearts about what we've been through and resolve ourselves to move past it, no matter what.

David made a decision. He knew he still had a wonderful life to live and a people who needed his kingly leadership, so he had reasons not to stay down for too long. He had reasons to live—many of them. He therefore wasn't going to allow blame or shame to weigh him down and prevent him from living the life God had called him to live. Knowing he could do nothing to reverse the situation, David made a decision to conclude his period of mourning for his son immediately after his death because he knew the worst was over and the best was yet to come.

David was able to have this mindset because he owned his mistakes immediately upon being called out on them. He knew he had done wrong and understood there was a price he was going to have to pay, a price for which he would have to mourn. And once he paid that price, he knew it was time to move on. Had David not had this mindset of owning his mistakes, he would have prolonged his mourning and not been able to find the peace he needed to continue living a prosperous life after a season of sin, selfishness, and bad decisions.

In using this scripture reference for this chapter, I want to clarify something so we don't miss the message here. I am not in any way saying that burning out in pastoral ministry is similar to the sins of lusting after a woman and having her husband killed in order to act on that lust. The primary reason for the comparison between David's sins and pastoral burnout is to illustrate the importance of owning your experiences so you can not just move on from them, but do so in victory. Just as David took ownership over the mistakes that led to the death of his infant son, I encourage you to take similar ownership, both over the various events that led to burnout, whether they were your fault or not, and over the fact that you burned out in the first place.

Suffering burnout can be humiliating because you feel like you're letting both God and people down, so you feel inclined to want to distance yourself from that season in your life. If you own that season, however, you will empower yourself to talk about it and prayerfully, position yourself to one day minister to others who have gone through what you've endured.

Taking ownership over a negative season in your life means coming to grips with it and, to a certain extent, getting over it. Getting over it doesn't mean you no longer feel upset about what you've been through; it simply means you've grown from it to the point where you feel comfortable talking about it and helping others in a similar situation. It means you no longer allow the situation to consume or control you.

Just as it's bad advice to tell someone who is 100 or more pounds overweight to lose weight, it's equally bad for someone to tell you, a recovering pastor, to just get over what you've been through and move on. Neither is good advice because each is rude, insensitive, and devoid of empathy or understanding. At some point, though, each absolutely needs to happen for long-term wellbeing. You'll never forget what happened, you'll never sweep it under the rug, and you may never be able to distance yourself from it in the court of public opinion, but at some point, no matter how long it takes, the pain of burnout won't sting quite as much as it used to. And when that happens, like King David, you'll be able to move on from it, minister to others, and live victoriously.

PRACTICAL APPLICATION

If you've endured the pain of pastoral burnout, then, in no uncertain terms, you've suffered a traumatic situation, and you are mourning (or have mourned) a significant loss. You're not only dealing with the loss of a title or position, along with whatever perks or benefits accompany that position, but you're grieving the loss of something very personal to you, and you need time and space to heal.

I would venture a guess that for most of us men and women of the cloth, we did not stumble into this ministry thing haphazardly. And for those of you not in ministry, you should have a baseline expectation that your pastor's decision to enter vocational ministry was not a hasty one, entered into without much prayer, preparation, and self-evaluation.

We did not wake up one Monday morning with the call to preach on our heart and start pastoring a church the following Sunday. Just as with anything serious, be it a personal savings plan, getting married, having children, starting a business, continuing your education, or even beginning a new fitness regimen, the process of answering the call to Christian ministry is more than a notion.

It's a call that takes time, costs money, requires further education, causes at least some level of isolation from your friends and peers, cuts deeply into your social life, leads to significant lifestyle changes, and oftentimes demands some amount of time away from your family.

In other words, answering the call to ministry is hard. And if that call requires becoming a pastor, it's even harder.

So, when this whole pastoring thing doesn't work out and leaves you hurt, scarred, scared about what your future holds, disillusioned, and completely distrusting of God and God's people, you absolutely have something to mourn.

I know I did.

Embracing an entirely different direction

As I've stated previously, when I resigned from pastoral ministry at the end of August 2013, I was a year and a half into a 3-year Doctor of Ministry program at Ecumenical Theological Seminary in Detroit. I knew from day one that I wanted to study the role of social media in building community and spiritual formation. And when I entered the program in January 2012 as the youngest Presiding Elder in African Methodism, I had every intention on doing my study in the context of the AME Church. I knew exactly what I wanted to do, how I was going to structure it, and whom I needed to talk to in order to make it happen.

But those were just my plans. God had something different for me, but it took time for me to embrace it.

When I stepped down from the pastorate, I did not relinquish my orders, but I did remove myself from all AME-related church services, activities, meetings, conferences, and fellowships. I didn't even answer phone calls from AME colleagues for a long time after my departure. What I had endured was so bad that I knew I needed a clean break from everything having to do with what I had just walked away from so I could clear my head, regain my footing, and maintain what bit of sanity I still had.

I therefore knew the convenient, cozy, tidy little doctoral project I had fabricated in my own mind was going to have to change. I made a few initial tweaks to make it ecumenical in scope, rather than focused squarely on AME initiatives and AME participants, and then started recruiting project participants based on my tweaks.

I had a difficult time reaching out to and recruiting complete strangers for this project, but I was able to come up with six people who were ready, willing, and enthusiastic about being a part of my study. Six was by no means a sizable number, but it was at least enough to put together a decent qualitative study if my analysis was strong.

With these six participants and with a good purpose and plan for my project, I went into my candidacy review two days before Thanksgiving 2013, confident about the proposal I had put together and comfortable with the overall direction of my study. I was ready to get on with the project, write and defend my dissertation, and begin the work of positioning myself in the world as a church communications professional.

But again, those were just my plans. God had something different for me, but it took time for me to embrace it.

That something different started at the candidacy review when the faculty member who was my committee chairperson at the time (before some personnel shifting took place) listened to my brief presentation and decided that I essentially needed to start over. The foundation for his decision was the fact I had started my presentation by listing several of the ubiquitous, well-known statistics on pastoral burnout, yet the rest of my material didn't have much of anything to do with the recovery from and eradication thereof.

In other words, I was willing to mention burnout in pastoral ministry as a reason pastors needed to come together and build community online, but I hadn't given thought to actually honing in on the subject of pastoral burnout to direct my research, formulate topics I would cover in my project, or choose participants for the project.

I was therefore asked to go back to the drawing board and update my proposal with a new focus on the subject of pastoral burnout. This updated scope would give new direction to the literature I researched, the participants I recruited, and the topics I discussed in community with those participants. I had to show my chairperson these changes in a new proposal before he would officially approve my candidacy.

When I received my "Go back to the drawing board" directive in that first candidacy review meeting, I was devastated because I had worked so hard to prepare myself and had thought I had put together a quality proposal for a meaningful project. I didn't want to start over. For all the work it had taken me to get to that point, I was being told it wasn't quite enough. It took me a couple weeks to pick myself up off the mat from this disappointment.

It wasn't until after updating and submitting that proposal, recruiting an entirely new group of participants, doing the project, writing the dissertation, and defending it did I discover how important it was for me to have dealt with that disappointment, for it produced something much greater than I could have ever imagined.

Owning your experience requires greater revelation

Had I been cleared to go with my original proposal, I would have put together a nice project with nice results, written a nice dissertation, and perhaps made a nice impact on the kingdom, but refocusing the scope of my project to deal head-on with the issue of burnout in pastoral ministry helped me to create something I know is far more relevant and believe will be far more impactful for the body of Christ.

The reason I had such a hard time at first accepting this potential for greater kingdom impact was not just because I had to start over, but even more so because I didn't want to be known as the "burnout guy".

I didn't enroll in the Doctor of Ministry program to become the "burnout guy". I entered to become a better ministry practitioner and position myself as an authority in the church communications space. I've been passionate about church communications for a long time, and I'm still making moves to become better equipped and more connected in the field.

Where I've found the blessings of God, however, has been in writing and speaking as passionately as possible on burnout. I don't see myself relenting on this subject anytime soon. But this passion I now have for ministering to burnt-out pastors and pastors looking to avoid burnout had to develop over time, starting first with my taking ownership of my burnout experience, as well as my mandate and responsibility to talk about it in every form and forum possible.

When I was asked to refocus my research on building community online to hone in on pastoral burnout, I, quite frankly, did not want to, not just because I thought it would be too hard or because I wanted to advance professionally in other areas, but because I had been looking at my burnout experience as something that simply happened to me, not as something that could possibly shape me and push me into my ultimate purpose.

Simply stated, until I received the greater revelation, I thought my burnout experience was merely a moment in time from which I could simply move on. But in my writing the articles for the LinkedIn burnout series and preparing to write this book, I have come to learn that my experience was not just a season of pain with which I was afflicted, but it was a season of refining and strengthening trial that I could leverage to minister to others, build community, and foster my own spiritual development.

Burnout doesn't have to be something you go through and hope to forget about. The greater story, the more impactful ministry here is if you use your burnout to propel your life and ministry forward. Come to grips with the fact that it happened, extract the lessons God wants to you to take away from the experience, and embrace your responsibility to tell others about it and help them avoid what you've gone through or heal from what they've been through.

And most importantly—here's where the power is—actually begin to take pride in what you've been through because if you're reading this right now, it means your trial didn't lead to your demise and that God is not through with you yet, meaning that no matter how bad things may be right now, better days are not many days hence.

Shame is of Satan. Don't ignore your burnout experience, own it. Embrace it. Minister through it! When I began to do this, everything changed for me. My prayer is that you will one day be able to testify to the same.

DEVOTIONAL POINTS
Reflect
1. Think of the worst thing you've been through regarding the burnout; then think about the fact that you're still here. It didn't kill you. You survived it. So you're more powerful than that. Be encouraged.
2. Consider what you'll be able to do with the rest of your life, whether you reenter full-time ministry or not, if you allow yourself to get past what you've been through, if you allow God to lift that weight from your shoulders. Think about what you'll be able to do without that extra weight and burden. Think of the lives you can impact for Christ. What is all of that worth to you?

Read
1. 2 Samuel 11-12
2. Blog post, "Does 'Just Get Over It' Actually Work? Thoughts on Overcoming Burnout," by Steve Bagi, a guest poster on ExPastors.com. For the sake of transparency, I will mention that I read this article for the first time only days before I penned these words, and I only know of its existence because the Holy Spirit brought it back to my remembrance. What I appreciate about this excerpt is how incredibly candid and honest he is about the true plight of pastoral burnout, having endured it himself. Thankfully, he doesn't offer a lot of the trite "A burnt-out pastor just needs a little more Jesus" type answers indicative of one who hasn't been through burnout, and for that reason alone, the post is worth a read.

Pray
#PrayForYourPastor
During my year of hell with the church from which I resigned from pastoral ministry, my Bishop scheduled a late-night meeting with my members and me, following evening worship at one of our district meetings. The room in which we met was as divided as the congregation had been that entire conference year, with one side totally against me, and

the other side, willing to fight with me and for me until the end. After comments went back and forth between factions for at least 30 minutes, it was very clear what one of the core problems was. And that problem was that a number of people would not even afford me the opportunity to be their pastor. They didn't accept me from day one and therefore, they magnified and publicized every mistake I made.

Now, witnessing this dynamic didn't give the Bishop impetus to help me in any way moving forward, not even with a vote of confidence in the man who had just been his Presiding Elder. What he did do, though, was tell a brief story about the first or second church he pastored when he was still in his 20s. He told of how his people loved him so much that they were understanding of him and just laughed it off when he walked past the church Saturday morning in casual clothes just a few minutes before the start of a wedding he was supposed to officiate. He had simply forgotten. The whole thing was a misunderstanding easily rectified, but the people loved him enough to be understanding and extend grace. Unfortunately, that story fell upon half a room of deaf ears.

Pray you can give your pastor that same understanding and patience with all he/she goes through on a regular basis. Your pastor will be so much better, so much more effective without all that added pressure that comes from extra scrutiny.

My prayer for you...

Father, in Jesus' name, give your recovering servants a David-like experience of peace with the events of their past. Put them in contact with the most loving, encouraging, life-affirming, positive-speaking people who will minister to them in this season and guide them into a place where getting over it is indeed possible. And when the enemy would try to stagnate your people by keeping fresh the memory of things that have long since been thrown in the sea of forgetfulness, help your servants to recognize the attack, fight it, and defeat it, by the power of your Spirit. May your people, even as they read these words now, be supernaturally healed at the level of their emotions so they can be free to continue their rebuilding process and live abundantly, from this moment forward. This I pray in Jesus' name, Amen.

IV
REBUILD YOUR LIFE

After the psyche, foundation, and faith of the recovering pastor have been rebuilt, or at least worked on significantly, he or she can start putting the pieces of his or her life back together. The goal in this rebuilding journey, as stated in the title of this book, is to renew and restore the burnt-out pastor, and everything that has been covered thus far is building toward that goal. The focal areas of this section of the journey are all geared toward helping the man or woman of God regain confidence and get comfortable living again, for God is not through with him or her yet. No one can be completely sure what life will look like post-burnout, but what is desired for the recovering pastor is that he or she is able to resume a productive, God-glorifying life, inside or outside of ministry, whatever that may look like.

CYLAR

-10-
STORY
How will you be defined?

"When Judas, his betrayer, saw that Jesus was condemned, he repented and brought back the thirty pieces of silver to the chief priests and the elders. He said, "I have sinned by betraying innocent blood." But they said, "What is that to us? See to it yourself." Throwing down the pieces of silver in the temple, he departed; and he went and hanged himself."
Matthew 27:3-5

THEOLOGICAL REFLECTION

As alluded to briefly in Chapter 8, comparing the actions, fates, and legacies of Peter and Judas tells you all you need to know about the importance of taking control of the story you tell with your life. The actions of these two of the original twelve disciples of Jesus were very similar, but because what was in their hearts was different, the course of their lives went in two completely different directions, and the legacies they left behind after death were as opposite as night and day.

The actions of these two disciples can be considered very similar because both men essentially sold Jesus out. Yes, only Judas' betrayal involved actual money exchanging hands, but if you consider how you would feel if someone whom you were close to—remember, Peter was one of the three out of the group of twelve who was really close to Jesus—denied to multiple people, multiple times having any association with you whatsoever, I imagine you would feel betrayed and like you had been sold out.

While their actions were similar, these men experienced vastly different fates. Matthew's (26:75) and Luke's (22:62) passion narratives each record Peter walking away and weeping bitterly upon hearing the cock crow and realizing that, as Jesus had predicted, Peter had indeed denied Him three times. But in Chapter 21 of John's gospel, when Jesus appeared to the disciples before His ascension, He took time to talk to Peter and restore him. On the surface, it appears as if Jesus was simply frustrating Peter by continuing to ask him if he loved Jesus, but what was happening here was Jesus was letting Peter know he still had work to do. His ministry was nowhere near complete, and God was not through with him yet.

Peter was an intensely emotional man, and I'm sure it devastated him to know that he betrayed Christ when the chips got down, but Jesus understood that and knew Peter needed his confidence restored and needed to be at his best for the work that was still before him, the work we see with the growth of the first-century Christian church in Acts.

Judas, on the other hand, was never sincere about serving Christ, so upon realizing the error of his ways, he could think of no better action than to run off and hang himself. In Matthew 27:3-4, Judas appears to have the same level of contrition concerning his wrongdoing as Peter did, but since his heart had always been oriented toward greed and deception, Judas lost all hope after realizing the consequences of his betrayal. As one of the twelve, he walked with Jesus and observed all he did throughout his earthly ministry, yet he must not have picked up anything along the way that could have encouraged him in a time like this.

Perhaps Judas thought about the last supper and how Jesus said very plainly that He knew Judas was going to betray him (Matthew 26:23-25), or about how Jesus immediately knew the reason Judas kissed Him (26:50). Maybe Judas weighed these events in his mind against the contents of his heart and realized that, for good reason, Jesus never trusted him, and because of that, Judas may have believed he had absolutely nothing to live for and no hope for repentance after realizing the consequences of his actions.

Both disciples betrayed their leader, committing actions for which they each felt a high level of remorse. But because of what was in their hearts, each processed that devastation and reacted to it differently. One gave himself a chance to be remembered for something other than the worst thing he had ever done, and the other aborted that chance by killing himself. Peter took control of his story and after Jesus restored his confidence, he went on to do great work for the kingdom of God. Judas, on the other hand, allowed his story to control him and by killing himself, ensured that for all time, the very first thing anyone would say about Judas was that he was a betrayer. By killing himself, Judas guaranteed that he would always be remembered for the lowest point in his life.

In the ebbs and flows of this tumultuous journey of life, we're going to endure some seasons and do some things we'll be ashamed of and would rather never talk about ever again if we had it our way. The problem is we don't have it our way, especially if what we went through that we're trying to take attention away from happened in a very public, humiliating fashion. We cannot prevent people who don't have our best interests at heart from talking about us, but we do have the power to change the narrative by taking ownership over the worst events of our lives and committing to making powerful ministry out of them. If we place our emphasis more on what the future will bring than what mistakes we made in our past, then our focus will be on accomplishing something far greater that will give people something to talk about.

When we take responsibility for the story we tell about our burnout experience and, rather than wallowing in it or pretending it didn't happen, decide to use it as a springboard to greater, then we let the world know that we're no longer going to allow the shame and embarrassment we feel from what we've been through to keep us from living abundantly, whatever that looks like moving forward. And you let the enemy know that no one can define you or your legacy but God, no matter how rough a go you've had of it.

Even more powerfully than that, when we petition the help of the Holy Spirit and muster up the courage to tell our story, we become even greater kingdom builders because we're offering ourselves up to be vulnerable for the sake of God's glory. We are courageously sharing our story so that many can know they are not alone in their struggle and many others can be prepared for or even prevent the pitfalls that ensnared us during our burnout experience.

In other words, when we tell our story, we take authority of our lives back from the enemy and we proactively minister through our pain for the benefit of others. And when we do so, we move one step closer in our rebuilding process. That is exactly what Peter did and what Judas didn't have the heart to do, and we remember them differently because of it.

PRACTICAL APPLICATION

I officially made my decision to step down from pastoral ministry at the Michigan Annual Conference, one year after receiving the assignment. It was clear that this was the decision I absolutely had to make, but before I did so, I met with my Bishop to ask him one very important question. In my mind, the decision had long been made, but I just wanted his answer to my question as confirmation of that decision.

He answered it exactly how I thought he would, so the next words out of my mouth were that I was stepping down, not just from the helm of that church, but from itinerant ministry altogether. I was unwilling to go to another church and potentially find myself in the same oppressive situation again. I couldn't put my family through that a second time. So, I essentially said to the Bishop, "Thank you, but no thank you."

I needed healing. It was crystal clear to me that I was not

going to be retained at this church and would have to transition to another congregation in consecutive years. My potentially moving again was one of the most important reasons for my decision to step down. As Bishop TD Jakes has so eloquently preached and taught on in the past, we as pastors often bleed while we lead, but I was completely unwilling to leave a trail of blood from my current assignment to the next one.

It would have been completely irresponsible of me to take my issues, my hurts, my pains, my depression, my ever-growing distrust for the leadership over me in this context from one church to another. The people deserve to have a man or woman of God to care for their souls who is completely unencumbered by any outside distractions or external forces. You won't find a pastor anywhere who isn't dealing with something, but there are plenty of healthy leaders whose minds and hearts are clear enough to be able to focus squarely on the most arduous but rewarding task of winning souls to Christ.

For all these reasons, the clear choice, the responsible choice, the right choice was for me to resign from pastoral ministry and remove myself from the pool of itinerant elders eligible to lead a church. I wasn't relinquishing my orders; I was simply taking time to heal and to reevaluate my direction in ministry.

It was a bold, costly step financially, but it was a necessary one. And most importantly, it was a choice I made, free from pressure or influence from anyone. I was writing my own story and charting my own path, and I wasn't going to let anyone do either for me.

Or so I thought.

Taken out of my hands

I had my meeting with the Bishop on a Wednesday afternoon. We presented our annual report to the conference Thursday morning. It was my intention to schedule a meeting with my people—those in the church who fully supported my family and me every step of the way—some time between that morning and Saturday afternoon to let them know we loved and appreciated them, but I had to resign and move on.

It was going to be a tough conversation, it was going to be an emotional conversation, but it was one my wife and I were prepared to have with our people on our terms. They deserved that. While many talked about, prayed against, and sabotaged us at every turn, these people supported us, encouraged us, helped us with our children, enthusiastically embraced the vision, and were an absolute joy to pastor.

My wife said it best in a goodbye message on social media shortly after our departure. We fell in love with these people, and not only would they always be in our hearts, but we would absolutely remain in touch with them. A couple weeks after we left, we had our youngest daughter's first birthday party, and many of them drove down to celebrate with us. For consecutive months following that, two of my young people celebrated birthdays of their own, and we were there.

To this day, we still talk to many of our old members regularly, not about anything going on at the church (that would be inappropriate), but simply about life in general, because to us, they are family.

So, we knew we owed it to them to inform them of my decision to step down. Unfortunately, that decision was taken out of my hands, as the Bishop made the announcement on the conference floor immediately after I presented our annual report. He had his reasoning for doing this, and I don't criticize it, but had I known he would even think about doing that, I would have simply requested, upon meeting with him, that he not say anything about it but give me the opportunity to meet with my members in private and share the news with them.

At that moment, I felt my story had been taken from me because I was not given the chance to tell the story myself. It's difficult to backtrack and retroactively explain yourself once information has been shared and the damage already done. My final moment as Pastor ended abruptly with a quick, unexpected announcement, stripping me of the ability to shape my story the way I wanted to shape it.

I wanted to share with my supporters three very important things:

1. I was NOT quitting, but I had to move on. I was burnt out, and they deserved a pastor who was not.
2. People and forces beyond my control had compromised my ability to pastor them effectively. I was not being retained anyway. My supporters had nothing to do with my departure.
3. I enjoyed being their pastor, I loved them, and would always love them.

Since I was not afforded the opportunity to have this conversation with them myself, I could not share these sentiments with them, so everyone was free to draw their own conclusions from the announcement.

This was the nail in the coffin to bury what had been a bitter twelve months.

The importance of story

Now is the right time to tell this story in this forum. Doing so in 2013 or 2014 would have been too soon, and telling it immediately after my resignation would have led to my bleeding all over the screen. Two months before I resigned, I knew I would one day tell this story, but the timing absolutely had to be right.

This story is too important, too relevant, too resonant with too many people for me to show bad stewardship over this story by telling it out of turn.

I am not the first pastor who has ever dealt with intense conflict in a church, and I'm not the first pastor to experience burnout in ministry. And unfortunately, I certainly won't be the last, as statistics state that 1,500-1,800 servants depart from the pastorate each and every month. That is why I knew I needed to tell this story.

The process of rebuilding a pastor from a place of despair back to a place of confidence, productivity, and victory in

Christ Jesus, whether that place is in ministry or outside of ministry, is a lengthy, multifaceted, multi-step process that involves shaping or reshaping the pastor's story.

What story? What story are we reshaping and retelling? What story do we need to take ownership of and tell in the way that best serves us and the people we serve?

In chapter 9, we discussed taking ownership specifically over the burnout experience. Because of who you represent as a man or woman of the cloth, burnout in ministry can cause a level of embarrassment in one's life. At least, that's what the experience did to me. So much so that I didn't want to become "that guy" who preaches and teaches on burnout.

I'm so much more than one season in my life, and I didn't want that season to define my ministry moving forward. It wasn't until I understood the blessing in being "that guy", at least in part, and understanding how many lives I could bless in the process that I owned my burnout experience and embraced my mandate to share it as often as possible.

The story I'm focusing on here, however, is your overall story. You have to think through and discern how your burnout experience fits in the story of your life. This goes for anyone, whether you're in ministry or not—what you've been through doesn't define you, nor does it limit you, unless you let it.

Appropriating our past

There are concrete lessons you take from the negative seasons in your past, and then there are a number of useless memories that have no place in your life if you wish to move forward.

Useless not from the standpoint that they don't matter or that what you've been through is somehow invalid, but rather from the standpoint that those experiences don't have any control of who you are or who you will be moving forward.

Dan Sullivan, one of the world's foremost coaches of entrepreneurs, says that the role your past has in your future is the role you assign to it. You have dominion over your past. You and you alone get to decide what from your past stays in your past and what part of it you carry with you into your future. In the context of rebuilding the pastor from the pain of burnout in ministry, you demonstrate that dominion over your past by deciding to take with you the lessons you've learned and the insights you've gained about yourself and about life, and you leave behind you the pain, the mistakes, the negativity, and the depression it caused.

It is our job to process everything we've been through in this life and do one of two things with it as we move forward—leave it behind or take it with us. The problem we run into internally is that we try to make our past a both-and proposition, rather than an either-or one, which is what it really is. We cannot take both the lessons and the pain from our past experiences with us; we can either take one or the other.

Nor can we take every memory from the past with us. Those memories that do nothing but tear us down and cause us to see ourselves less than how God sees us can't come with us, but those memories, whether of triumphs or trials, that work to affirm who we are in Christ and remind us of the value we have to share with the world can come with us.

Learning how to properly process our past is key to crafting an impactful story because we don't want the focus of our story to be on a series of negative events from which the reader or hearer will walk away saying:

"Dang, that was tough!"

Instead, we want that reader or hearer to internally experience our story with us as we share it, and, most importantly, walk away from it encouraged about it to the point where he or she says:

"Dang, that was tough…but look at God!"

Huge difference.

How I'm reshaping my story

Needless to say, the objective in sharing my burnout

experience is the latter, not the former, but had I started talking too early, before I had a chance for God to heal me, before I had an opportunity to build community with others around the shared experience of burnout, the former is exactly what you would have gotten.

I know that now is the right time to talk openly and extensively about burnout in pastoral ministry because I fully understand how what I've been through fits in the overall story of my life and my purpose in ministry now and beyond.

I was blessed to have the opportunity to go through a Doctor of Ministry program that taught us how to reflect theologically on our lives and how they inform our ministry passion and the course of our research. We did this in the form of a spiritual autobiography, which is the second chapter of every dissertation written by a graduate of our program.

Not everyone who goes through burnout is blessed to have done so while matriculating through a DMin program, so it is my prayer that I will soon have the opportunity to lead burnt-out pastors through crafting a spiritual autobiography and processing what they've been through and how it informs their lives and ministries moving forward.

I know my decision to leave how and when I did will always be viewed by many as that of a young man who was wet behind the ears and decided to quit because it got too hard. I used to get upset about that characterization, but I don't anymore because I have the power and ability to tell my story the way I want to. I'm taking control of my story and reshaping it for God's glory.

I'm reshaping my story from something horrific to something hopeful.

I'm reshaping my story from something painful to something promising.

I'm reshaping my story from one that dwells on the negative to one that accentuates the positive.

I'm reshaping my story by no longer approaching it as a series of "They did this to me, and it was horrible" anecdotes, and instead, looking at it from an "I went through this, but I'm stronger, wiser, and better now because of it" point of view.

When we can begin to shift our perspective about what we've been through in this way, we can begin the process of rebuilding our lives after burnout. There's victory on the other side of defeat, joy on the other side of pain, sunshine after rain, but we have to embrace the process, take control of our story, and assume sound stewardship over it to realize that other side.

And once we do so, our lives can take off again.

DEVOTIONAL POINTS
Reflect
1. Think about your story. Dwell on it. Analyze your burnout experience top to bottom, as closely as you possibly can without depressing yourself. Then, start telling your story as often as you possibly can—in your private journal, on your personal blog, on someone else's blog as a guest, on yours or someone else's podcast, on your on web show, or just recorded on your smartphone for no one's eyes or ears but yours.

Master that story and become one with it, like you would an elevator pitch for a new business, product, or job. You'll have plenty opportunities at some point in time to share your burnout experience, and when they come, you'll be prepared to tell the most powerful, heartfelt, relevant story possible because you've taken ownership of that story, and people will resonate with and appreciate that ownership.

I've had a number of opportunities to share my story in the year and a half between my departure from pastoral ministry and the publishing of this book, and in that time, I can't begin to tell you how many people have told me how much my willingness to share has blessed them. Every such message I receive is a blessing from God that propels me forward and encourages me to stay on this path. Such affirmation is powerful beyond measure and has made all of this worthwhile. And it's available to you, too, if you begin telling your story.

2. If you're reading this right now and you're at the point where you're even casually entertaining the thought of ending your life, please consider Judas for a few minutes. Yes, Judas was a deceiver and a betrayer who had an impure heart toward the one he was supposed to be following. But had he committed to turning his life around, he would have found forgiveness and could have been positioned to render powerful service for the kingdom of God during the first century Christian church expansion.

Think about everything you could disqualify yourself from if you end your life right now. Consider all the people who have gone through or are currently going through what you've endured and how much they could possibly benefit from hearing someone else's story and knowing they are not alone. Take ownership of your experience and take authority over your story and tell it. Don't abort the gift God has still placed inside you!

Read

1. Matt 27:3-5; John 21:15-24.
2. *The Wounded Minister* by Guy Greenfield. Much in line with Rediger's *Clergy Killers*, as discussed in Chapter 2, Greenfield talks about deceptive lay members who deliberately undermine the pastor's ministry to stay in control of the church and make sure their needs are met. Greenfield gets much more personal and candid with his story, though, almost uncomfortably so. But it's a good kind of uncomfortable that will really make you reconsider your perspective on some issues. It's a must-read for the helpful layperson, the sabotaging layperson, and the rebuilding pastor.

Pray
#PrayForYourPastor

Your pastor is working as hard as he or she possibly can

to implement the vision he or she has received from God for the ministry. A vision is never easy to implement, as there are bumps and bruises along the way, and interpersonal and/or community conflicts are likely to occur at times. Pray that you as a committed layperson, as well as your fellow church members, will both hold your pastor accountable and be as understanding as possible when he or she falls short.

Your pastor is doing the best job he or she can do, and with your prayers and your help, he or she will continue to do so. You can really help shape the story of your church in a powerful way by how you frame things. Yes, hold your pastor's feet to the fire lovingly, honestly, and respectfully, but help keep your pastor encouraged by reminding him or her of the positive things taking place in the church and celebrating those accomplishments as often as possible. When the story of the ministry focuses more on accentuating the positive than dwelling on the negative, your pastor will be less likely to buckle and burnout under the pressures pervasive in ministry.

My prayer for you…

Father, encourage your rebuilding servants right now, in Jesus' name. Help your people to take ownership of their story and develop within them the courage to tell it whenever and wherever possible so people who need to hear it can be blessed by it. Expose your rebuilding servants to videos, podcasts or other audio programs, websites, books, and other materials from people who know how to tell a story in a way that captures and compels people. May your servants take notes from these stories and apply them to their own story so they can tell it effectively and minister powerfully.

Help your recovering, rebuilding servants to look deep within themselves and bless them with the emotional fortitude to deal with the biggest, most embarrassing aspects of their burnout experience, and bring divine healing to every area of their lives so they will be empowered to share their story boldly and confidently for your glory. In the name of

Jesus I pray these things, Amen.

-11-
REINVENTION
God is not through with you yet

"And I said, "Lord, they themselves know that in every synagogue I imprisoned and beat those who believed in you. And while the blood of your witness Stephen was shed, I myself was standing by, approving and keeping the coats of those who killed him.' Then he said to me, 'Go, for I will send you far away to the Gentiles.'"
Acts 22:19-21

THEOLOGICAL REFLECTION

The statistic is well-known. It's everywhere. It's right in your face. 1,500 pastors leave vocational ministry every single month. And that number is permanent. People who leave ministry often do not return, and that is one trend, along with (of course) the number of pastors burning out and resigning, I'm specifically working to eradicate. This issue of permanent resignation is why reinvention is such a vital step in the rebuilding process for the recovering pastor. What does the pastor who spent years investing time, talent, and treasure into his or her calling from God do after burnout? How does such a person reinvent him/herself?

When I consider examples of what it means to reinvent oneself, I think instantly of the original 12 disciples of Jesus Christ and I think of the apostle Paul. Paul's story is particularly compelling because of how much shame he had about what he had done before the Lord called him and how he channeled that shame and turned it into powerful ministry for Jesus Christ.

Acts 21 records Paul being arrested in the temple in Jerusalem after he traveled there against the passionate pleas of the men who traveled and ministered with him, but with the approval and by the direction of the Holy Spirit. Those who followed Paul were fearful of his traveling there because while there were plenty of Jewish Christians in Jerusalem, there were many more who were zealous for the law of Moses, just as Paul once was, and therefore would not approve of his being there because of how well-known he had become for preaching Christ.

It was obvious that Paul was going to suffer the fate he did because of his reputation, yet he had no fear whatsoever in going to Jerusalem. When he was arrested in the temple, he was immediately taken away and beaten until the ranking military officer, the tribune, saw him and ordered him to be chained and brought to the barracks for questioning, at which point Paul shared the testimony of his conversion. In his sharing, it was important for Paul to state and restate that he was a Jew and to give his testimony in the Hebrew language.

What's most significant to me about his testimony and what's most relevant to the subject of reinvention is what Paul said about his commission from Jesus in a vision to leave Jerusalem and go preach Christ to the Gentiles. Jesus told Paul to get out of Jerusalem quickly because the people would not accept Paul's testimony about Him, but Paul appeared to be focused on the question of why Jesus would even call Paul to share a testimony in the first place. Jesus was telling Paul to leave Jerusalem for a place where he could preach Christ, while Paul was seemingly asking why he would even be preaching Christ in the first place, given his background. Paul believed his background disqualified him from having anything to say on behalf of Christ, while Jesus essentially tried to convince Paul that it was his background that actually prepared him to minister on Christ's behalf.

Jesus had a work for Paul to do, and once Paul could get over his past, he figured out that his past uniquely qualified him to do that work. Once Paul got saved, he had to reinvent himself because he was no longer going to be the chief Pharisee, the chief persecutor and abuser of Christians, as he himself had become a Christian. Paul had to realize that persecuting Christians wasn't the essence of who he was. What was at his core was arguing for and defending something passionately; Paul just needed his perspective adjusted a little bit so he could argue and defend for the right reasons. At his core, Paul was a master teacher and motivator. Once Paul connected with his purpose, he took that same passion he had for persecuting Christians and translated it into finding Christians, converting them and discipling them in the faith. Once Paul found out was he was truly meant to do, his life had meaning, his life took off, and we have two-thirds of the New Testament today because of it.

Now, when it comes to reinventing the recovering, rebuilding pastor and rediscovering life after burnout, it's a little more difficult. Perhaps you've dedicated your entire adult life to ministry, and all of your marketable skills, formal education, and work experience up to the point of your burnout have been in ministry. You still have years to work. What do you do to pivot? Do you pivot at all?

As you are in this all-important step of reinventing yourself after burnout, you have to figure out what your life is going to look like moving forward. Are you looking to reenter full-time ministry as a lead or senior pastor after this brief respite, or would you rather serve as an associate pastor or in another ministry capacity on a church staff? Do you know you just need to leave vocational ministry altogether and want to leverage your ministry skills and experience to transition into a secular position? What do you love to do? Where is your sweet spot?

For you and your relationship with Christ, does walking away from pastoral ministry permanently mean walking away from your life's calling? If not, where do you see yourself going? In what direction do you feel the Lord leading you? If so, and you know without a doubt that quitting the pastorate permanently would mean completely walking away from the will of God for your life, how much of a break do you need from ministry in order to heal and prepare yourself to one day reenter? What do you need to do in the meantime for gainful employment and/or professional development until you heal sufficiently?

These are all questions you need to answer for yourself, but the answers are nowhere near cut and dry. I'd be lying to myself and to you if I pretended like they were.

At this most crucial step in the rebuilding process, consider Paul. When the Spirit hit him, he reinvented himself and pivoted into purpose. Before the blood of Jesus found him, he was the preeminent persecutor of Christians in all the land. After Paul's conversion experience, he submitted to what was already on the inside of him and became the most passionate preacher and productive pastor of all the first century apostles. At his core, Paul was a master motivator, and he stayed true to that core, before and after salvation. If you can find out what your core is, you can also pivot successfully. And success is available to you because God is not through with you yet.

PRACTICAL APPLICATION

Over 50 percent of current pastors state they would leave full-time vocational ministry if they were confident they had another way to make a living. That means at least every other pastor currently in ministry is hanging on to their position merely to keep food on the table and clothes on their families' backs.

The scariest thing about this most discouraging statistic is that, just as with any survey, people lie, especially when they're ashamed to reveal the real answer to the question they've been asked. That 50 percent could therefore actually be much higher.

Similar work, much different pay

Answering the call to not just preach the gospel but specifically to pastor, more than most professions, requires truly going all-in. Yes, there are a few fields where the graduate coursework may be more rigorous than ministry—law, engineering, business (depending on where you go)—but the length of time required to complete the coursework is very similar, only to make far less money. Only medicine requires more schooling than does professional ministry.

Obtaining a Juris Doctorate takes the same three years as a Master of Divinity, yet the JD graduate, especially after passing the bar exam in the state(s) of his or her choosing, emerges with far greater earning potential in the short term and long term than the MDiv grad does.

An engineering graduate is already coming out of undergrad with the potential to earn a far greater yearly income in his or her first job than the vast majority of pastors will ever make in a year, even with decades of experience. Completing a 1- or 2-year graduate engineering program only boosts that earning potential and income disparity.

An MBA student attends an 18-month to 2-year graduate program that boots his or her earning potential to above $100,000 annually, a salary very few pastors in this country will ever earn, again, even after decades of service. In half the time as the MDiv student, the MBA student will set him or herself up for a far more secure life for his or her family.

Furthermore, and more importantly for this discussion, graduates of these secular programs set themselves up not just to earn more money than full-time pastors, but to be more attractive in the job market and have many more options for employment.

Even when the full-time pastor decides to further his or her education and pursue a Doctor of Ministry, he or she will most likely still not earn close to the same money or have as many career options as an attorney, a corporate executive, or an engineer. Only with a PhD does the pastor truly open him or herself up to greater opportunities, most specifically, teaching in seminary.

I actually believe the DMin graduate can leverage his or her degree to find or create teaching opportunities in the academy the same way the PhD graduate does, but most do not. Several areas of study in graduate theological education, especially in an MDiv program, can be better taught by practitioners than theoreticians, and DMin professors can fill in that gap quite well. I had DMins teaching several of my classes in both of the seminaries I attended.

In a job or career, you are compensated for fulfilling a set of responsibilities that are assigned a specific dollar value by the people or entities providing the payment. Employees are compensated for time served and retained year after year (or however often they are evaluated through a performance review) based on their results. The value of their work is assigned by the company for which they work.

Entrepreneurs are compensated solely on the results they provide their clients, regardless of the time spent. Entrepreneurs ascribe a dollar value to their own work, and the marketplace determines how accurate that value is by deciding how much work that entrepreneur gets.

Being a full-time pastor isn't much different from being a corporate employee or an entrepreneur from the standpoint of being compensated for a set of responsibilities that are assigned a dollar value, in this case, set by the church.

Where pastoring is different than any other line of work is that you have responsibility over people's spiritual wellbeing, and compromising that wellbeing could have catastrophic ramifications for an entire community. In this way, being a pastor is so much more than just a job, so much so that one who is burnt out ought not remain in the position merely to collect a paycheck.

You can't just go through the motions as a pastor. It's a matter of life and death.

But that's what so many of them are forced to do everyday because of the various factors I shared above.

Going all-in

So, what is the point in all of this? Why am I comparing these different fields to that of ministry? I want to be very clear here. I'm not looking to get into a discussion about which graduate school is hardest, or costs the most money, or requires the most challenging entrance or certification exams.

I'm merely making the point that when someone decides to respond to the call God has placed on his or her life and attends seminary, he or she is certainly not making a financially motivated decision. He or she is leaving money and opportunity on the table and sacrificing everything to do what God has called him or her to do. For it's not the money, but it's the will of God and the growth of God's kingdom that he or she is after.

He or she is going all-in.

And going all-in for God should have its benefits, if not in the form of lucrative earnings, then at least in the form of peace of mind or career fulfillment. "The peace of God that surpasses all understanding" ought to be prevalent in the life of a pastor. Not to say that hard times won't come, but when they do, the support from our Heavenly Father ought to be enough to make the difference and pull us through.

So, how unbelievably discouraging it must be when that young pastor finishes seminary, finds a job that pays $30,000 per year, works 50- to 70-hour weeks, struggles to balance time between his or her family and the ministry, often takes the burden of an entire community upon him or herself, and yet is often unappreciated by the same people for whom he or she has sacrificed so much.

A pastor wears so many hats—motivational speaker, theologian in residence, visionary, teacher, counselor, hospital chaplain, accountant, chief fundraiser, community activist, maintenance person—yet is the first person whose job performance is questioned when anything goes wrong.

The pastor is every bit the professional that anyone else in the community is, yet he or she is the one professional who has a job everyone thinks they can do. No one tells the doctor, lawyer, or accountant how to do his or her job, but many people have constant commentary about what the pastor should or should not be doing on any given day.

In all of these ways, a pastor truly goes all-in, sacrificing everything to do his or her job at the highest level, often for an unappreciative people who either have no clue of the rigors of pastoral ministry or simply do not respect the office of the pastor the same way they do other professionals.

For women in ministry, the disrespect for the office is only heightened.

So, when the pastor who's gone all-in suffers burnout, and the same denomination or religious governing body who provided training or ordination for that pastor has zero systems or programs in place to support and coach him or her through the burnout season, the man or woman of God is left out in the cold with no one to turn to but God for help.

Now, don't get me wrong, I'm a living witness that, as renowned gospel artist Vickie Winans famously sang many years ago, "As long as [you] got King Jesus, [you] don't need nobody else!" He will heal you, He will deliver you, and He will set you free, but what exactly does that mean professionally?

What happens to the pastor after burnout? That's the central question this book has been trying to answer. Whether that pastor is looking to reenter full-time vocational ministry or not, he or she still needs to figure out what to do to support him or herself financially in the season of transition.

And since that pastor has gone all-in over a number of years to fulfill the calling of God on his or her life, reinventing him or herself, either on a transitional basis as he or she recovers, or as a permanent career change, is very difficult.

I have seen very well-educated, Doctorate-degreed pastors struggle to find secular work after burnout, not because they are not smart enough to do anything else, but because the job market, quite frankly, just does not value work experience within religious institutions as anything that can be transferred into other lines of work.

Many pastors have lots of experience balancing budgets, building teams, managing personnel, developing and executing strategic plans, and overseeing marketing campaigns—the kinds of job functions that could add value to any company. Hiring managers and interviewers, unfortunately, don't see that value and are instantly turned off when they see that experience is in the church.

It's as if putting a steeple atop a building automatically invalidates the professional value of anything that happens within it.

I certainly went all-in

I write all of this from personal experience, as I know intimately the disappointment of going all-in, burning out, and finding it difficult to translate all of my education into gainful employment outside of ministry.

After earning two bachelor's degrees from Morehouse College and the Georgia Institute of Technology (Georgia Tech) in December 2005, I made the trek back to Detroit from Atlanta for no other reason than because that's what the Lord instructed me to do. It was a road traveled by none of my peers, and it certainly wasn't a good decision for me professionally, as I was coming home to a job market that was literally frozen in the midst of the steep decline of the Big Three automakers.

Nobody was hiring. With my electrical engineering degree from a top-five engineering institution, the only full-time job I could obtain was at a parts inspection company, making $8.50 an hour. Unfortunately, by the time the professional job market finally picked back up in Michigan, I had been out of engineering school so long I was no longer attractive to potential employers.

With each passing year, it became increasingly difficult to explain the professional, non-church employment gaps in my resume. A byproduct of the decline of the automotive industry, my engineering career ended before it ever started.

What sustained me, though, was knowing that becoming an engineer was not the reason the Lord called me home to Detroit. God directed me home to begin my life and ministry, and I had to trust everything would come together in due time. I returned home with the intent of being a well-paid engineer attending seminary, but, as evidenced by my employment struggles, God wanted the primary emphasis to be on seminary and not a job.

I went all-in on a life of ministry and left piles of money on the table.

I started the MDiv program, met my wife, got ordained, got married, began pastoring, graduated, got ordained again, became the youngest Presiding Elder in the African Methodist Episcopal Church, got transferred to another church, and burned out, all within a 7-year period after going all-in.

Going all-in, unfortunately, proved disastrous for me the first go-around. I pushed all my chips toward the middle of the table and came up short. I lost my hand—a very valuable hand—and had to walk back home with my tail between my legs. But when I got home, I sat down with the manual, checked my pride at the front cover, and really figured out how to play the game.

I'm ready now for another hand, a new game. I don't know who I'm playing with this time around or where the game is being played, but I'm ready for the challenge. I'm ready to be productive and useful again in the world. I'm where every burnt-out pastor finds him or herself after a season of soul searching and rebuilding.

One very crucial point must be made here. When the burnt-out pastor reaches this point of readiness to once again provide great value in the world, it absolutely does not mean that he or she is ready to return to pastoral ministry. Statistically speaking, the average length of an entire pastorate is only four years, so for the most part, the burnt-out pastor does not return to the pulpit, or if so, not to the big chair.

What I'm talking about is the process of attempting to figure out viable, fulfilling career options after burnout. Many struggle to get past this point. I certainly have, even though I've been working to create options for my family and me outside of ministry for a number of years.

How I'm reinventing myself

A year and a half into pastoral ministry, my wife and I started Cylar Consulting as a way to leverage our professional skills and passions to create income for ourselves outside of ministry. My wife works with various clients in space planning and organizing, as well as event planning and logistics. I am a technology and digital strategy consultant for churches and nonprofits, as well as a professional editor and proofreader for published authors, students, and small businesses.

I have long believed that the pastor who builds a viable business on the side benefits in two important ways. Firstly, this pastor is completely free to live and work with integrity and make sound ministry decisions that are never motivated by his or her bottom line. When a pastor and his or her family are financially stable outside of ministry, they can be more mentally and emotionally stable in ministry. The pressures and demands of pastoral ministry are difficult enough on their own without having to be concerned with financial troubles.

Now, I am absolutely NOT saying that pastors who do not build side businesses are incapable of having ministries of integrity because many pastors I respect greatly do so quite well. My claim is simply that it's easier to live without compromise when the man or woman of God has done the work to build something outside of the pastorate.

Secondly, when such an entrepreneurially minded pastor is not only able to earn good money outside the church, but can do so while still putting in the proper time to be faithful to God and to the people and programs within the church, he or she becomes far less susceptible to the whims of lay and leadership, both of whom ultimately hold the pastor's financial future in the palms of their hands.

At my previous charge, a number of displeased laypeople closed their purses and wallets and decided to deliberately not give out of their anger with me, in hopes that the leadership over me who made personnel decisions would remove me from the church as soon as possible. This leadership, fearful of what would happen to the district's overall bottom line if a church of our caliber didn't meet its obligations, ignored my cries for help when I needed them the most, sided with the concerns of the people, and did not support me in any way.

For years, I had always said that I never wanted my career and livelihood to be subjected to the opinions and tactics of people working for their own best interests. That is exactly what happened, though.

My wife and I started our business with the hope of setting ourselves up for long-term financial success beyond the pulpit. But life happened and we were unable to dedicate the kind of time necessary to build the business to the point where walking away from pastoral ministry wouldn't have been as big a financial burden as it ended up being.

From a financial standpoint, I absolutely have to reinvent myself because now that I'm no longer pastoring, at least in the short term, it means I'm not doing the same thing I was doing previously to make a living. I have to dig down deep into the well of skills I've built up over a lifetime of schooling and hard work.

Now that I've been away from pastoring for a year and a half, I'm reinventing myself by doing three things. One, I'm doubling down on my core competencies and more aggressively marketing my aforementioned consulting services and the relationships I've built with past clients to gain and retain several new clients this year.

Two, I'm using my DMin to find as many teaching, writing, and training opportunities as I possibly can. This may not be true for everyone, but for most DMins I've heard of, gone to school with, or interacted with on any level, they seem to be either very secure in their ministry careers, or they are headed toward the end of their long corporate careers and are ready to focus on their ministries with a terminal degree in hand and money in the bank as a retiree.

That simply is not my experience. Through a series of events, I, quite frankly, have found myself all the way back at step one from a career standpoint. I am starting from the bottom. I am therefore looking to leverage this DMin as a PhD and search for publications, research projects, conventions, and other presentations to which I can contribute.

From what I've read—correct me if I'm wrong—the latter portion of the PhD process has a significant career counseling component wherein the candidate's advisor helps him or her identify employment opportunities and prepare his or her dissertation for its first set of journal publications upon graduation. You simply don't see this type of advisement at the DMin level, as it's expected that graduates continue their ministry in the local church.

Since I do not have a local church ministry right now, I am looking to do different things with my education that have not been done before. I want to continue my research through funded projects. I want to share my research in scholarly journals. I want to do with a DMin what PhDs do with their education. Will it work? I'm not sure, but I'm going to give it my best shot because I'm hungry.

Three, I'm fully embracing my newfound calling to minister wherever I can, whenever I can, about recovering from and eradicating burnout in pastoral ministry. As I shared previously, I was very reluctant about honing in on the subject of burnout because I didn't want to be identified for the rest of my life by one season in my life. I have since done a complete 180. If I must be the "burnout guy" to maximize my opportunities for kingdom impact, then I no longer have a problem being that guy. It's all about glorifying God.

Yes, if you're keeping score, in answering the question of how I'm reinventing myself after burnout, I've just listed three seemingly very different things. This is the reality of someone who has experienced burnout and is not looking to reenter pastoral ministry anytime soon. My future, honestly, is up in the air right now, not because I have any doubt about whether or not I will be successful, but because I don't know where the success is coming from or what it's going to look like.

It's an exciting time in my life right now because regardless of what has or has not manifested yet, I'm very secure because I know who holds my future. Just like the old hymn says,

> *Many things about tomorrow*
> *I don't seem to understand;*
> *But I know who holds tomorrow,*
> *And I know who holds my hand.*

DEVOTIONAL POINTS

Reflect

As mentioned earlier in the chapter, it is absolutely imperative that you take considerable time to seek God and discern God's direction for your life at this point in your journey. If God makes it absolutely clear that God is not through with you yet as a pastor, then you'll need to start thinking about how to leverage your skills to find temporary secular work or to even start a side business while you get back on your feet spiritually. If not, think long and hard about your core competencies and what you like to do most and how you can use those skills and desires to pivot into another career or business. Again, there are no clear-cut answers here, so you're going to have to take your time and give this some lengthy consideration.

Read (or listen to or watch…)

1. Book, *Moving On, Moving Forward*, by Michael J. Anthony and Mick Boersma. This is a fantastic resource filled with useful information and practical steps for pastors in transition. The type of transition the authors are referring to

here, though, is that of leaving one ministry assignment in search of another. Although much of the information can apply to some of the issues that have been discussed here, it is important to note this book is not about pastors in transition out of full-time ministry into secular work, either for a season or permanently. Part 3: "Where Do You Want to Be?" comprising chapters 10-14, are most relevant to this book, especially chapter 13 on revising your resume.

2. Podcast, *The Portfolio Life*, by *New York Times* Bestselling author, Jeff Goins [1]. The description for the podcast states that, "Jeff Goins shares thoughts & ideas that will help you to pursue work that matters, make a difference with your art & discover your true voice!" So he's approaching the idea of vocation or calling as not one thing you mysteriously find that you do for 30 years or more before you retire, but rather as a collection of personal and professional experiences along the winding road of life that you piece together into a portfolio that comprises the span of your professional career.

The latter, if you haven't noticed, is the way things are going now in the 21st century and beyond. As it's his program, Jeff describes it much better than I do in episode 47 of the podcast, entitled, "The Seven Stages of Finding Your Calling." Every episode of the podcast has been excellent to me, but this episode in particular resonated with me very deeply. It's worth a listen.

3. TED Talk, "Flow, the secret to happiness," by positive psychologist Mihaly Csikszentmihalyi [2]. This great talk is over a decade old at the printing of this book, but it is still very much relevant. The psychologist talks about what flow state is, what kind of work gets you to that state, and how you feel once you get there. A must-watch for anyone in a career transition of any kind.

4. Speech excerpt, "Levels," by Dr. Eric Thomas, aka "ET The Hip Hop Preacher" [3]. Eric and his team have compiled excerpts from his greatest speeches over his career into a series of mixtapes. (See endnotes if you are unfamiliar

with the term "mixtape" [4].) On his second mixtape, *Greatness is Upon You*, he has a track entitled, "Levels," where he describes the decision all-time NBA legend Kobe Bryant made to force a draft-night trade from the Charlotte Hornets to the Los Angeles Lakers.

About Kobe's decision, Eric states that Kobe was destined for greatness, and even as a teenager just entering the NBA, he could already tell the Hornets organization was not in line with his values of being a champion. The point he was making in this message is that before you can become successful, before you can figure out what you want out of life, you first need to get a good idea in your mind of what you do not want. You may not always know what success and fulfillment look like for you when you're in transition, but knowing what they don't look like and having a good grasp of your non-negotiables in life is a good start. It's a very inspirational clip.

Pray
#PrayForYourPastor

With your pastor currently at the helm, he or she is obviously not in the season of reinvention, as far as it pertains to his or her ministerial career, and that's a good thing. But perhaps your church is at a place of stagnancy or you're simply overly comfortable with the way things are and have been for some time, and your pastor is feeling the nudge of the Holy Spirit to turn up the heat on a few things within the ministry so it can be positioned for long-term growth.

Regardless of the type of church or its demography, it's difficult to lead change at a place where things are comfortable and conflicts are few, but ensuring the ministry thrives for generations to come requires strapping your boots up every now and then and taking that treacherous walk from the comfortable center toward the anything-but-comfortable cutting edge. Pray for your pastor to have the courage to do just that and for you and your fellow church members to support his or her efforts to move to the cutting edge and explore new ideas and initiatives for the sake of the long-term success of the ministry.

My prayer for you...

In Jesus' name, Lord, I pray for your recovering and transitioning servants who have no idea whatsoever what the next 3-6 months are going to look like. They built lives and ministries off of trusting you, but now, at this point in their lives, they need you more than ever. Grant your people both patience and peace during this most challenging period. Reveal to them skills you've already given them that they can translate to other areas. As your servants reinvent themselves, awaken within them dreams from long ago that they never acted on but you never forgot.

Supernaturally provide the provision to meet the vision. And should it be your will that one, a few, or all of your servants reading this someday reenter pastoral ministry, do a divine work of healing within them and preparation to accept the mandate you still have over their lives. Whether inside or outside of vocational ministry, prepare the way for them even now and break up the fallow ground so that wherever you send them, whatever plans you yet have for them, whenever you transition them, the atmosphere will already be prepared for them to be successful. For your leaders, Lord, I pray this prayer in Jesus' name, Amen.

Reinvention

-12-
RE-ENGAGEMENT
It's time to begin again

"Simon, Simon, listen! Satan has demanded to sift all of you like wheat, but I have prayed for you that your own faith may not fail; and you, when once you have turned back, strengthen your brothers."
Luke 22:31-32

THEOLOGICAL REFLECTION

As the old saying goes, those who fail to learn from history are doomed to repeat it. Each of us, at some point, is called to be that history so that we can warn, teach, and, most importantly, encourage those coming behind us out of what we've been through.

As we discussed in Chapter 10, Peter and Judas each fell short and let Jesus down during the most crucial moments leading to his crucifixion, but only one of them had the heart, the faithfulness, and the determination to come back from that most devastating moment to build a great life and ministry. Jesus knew both of them were going to screw up royally, and He said as much on separate occasions, but He was keenly aware of Peter's sincerity toward Him and thus felt the need to pull Peter to the side and encourage him before he denied Him.

Jesus essentially said to Peter, *Look, Satan knows the gift within you and is working with all his might to steer you off course and rob you of that gift. I already know you're going to stumble and fall, and you're going to be devastated about it, but don't wallow in that devastation. Get up, dust yourself off, and then reach back and pull someone else up with you. It's in the reaching back that you're going to learn the most about me. It's in the reaching back that you're going to come most acquainted with my grace. It's in your reaching back that you will minister most powerfully under my anointing and draw the most people to me.*

Jesus wanted to let Peter know that he believed in him and trusted that he could do the work of ministry effectively, despite his imperfections. I submit to you that Jesus knew what was inside Peter, not just because of His divine insight, but because Peter spent time with Jesus. Peter was one of the three disciples Jesus could be seen with most often, so Jesus got a chance to really get to know him. He saw Peter in his element. He heard Peter passionately prove his loyalty when Jesus prophesied that Peter would deny him three times. Jesus saw Peter defend his friend's honor by cutting off the ear of a slave of the high priest who had Jesus arrested (John 18:10). Jesus saw how devastated Peter was after denying Him. He knew Peter's heart. So He had to take the opportunity to minister to him.

The most encouraging thing about this text is the hope it gives those of us who have been sincere about serving God and were as faithful as we could be over our ministry yet still suffered burnout. I'm of the belief that the vast majority of pastors, even the ones who suffer burnout, do the best they can in ministry but oftentimes just face seemingly insurmountable circumstances that cause them to lose heart. Most pastors take their job very seriously, and the ones who burn out just get discouraged and don't feel they have a way out or a way forward. If Jesus could look into our hearts and see what He saw in Peter, I can imagine He'd have the same conversation with us: Look son (or daughter), I know you burned out and you feel like a failure, but I can use your fall for my glory. You're still here and you're still breathing, so you're not disqualified. Take a breather, get up, dust yourself off, and continue living. There are still so many out there who need your gift, who need your ministry. Don't give up!

What Jesus essentially told Peter before being denied, betrayed, and crucified and what He wants us to know today is that what we go through is not for ourselves. Our triumphs and our disappointments are not just for us to enjoy or to lament over, but they are designed to help pull out of us what is necessary to help those who have yet to traverse the path we've already tread. We would therefore be better served to flip our concept of discouragement on its head and look at it not as a reason to walk away from God and from God's people, but as an impetus to dig in, deal with it head on, and apply the lessons from it to do powerful ministry in the future, wherever that ministry may take place.

I've heard it said that burnout in pastoral ministry is the result of our giving the devil too much room in our lives. For countless reasons, as have been laid out throughout this book, we know by now, the issue of pastoral burnout is far too complex and multifaceted to explain it so simplistically. But for the sake of argument, let's consider that those of us who have suffered burnout did indeed allow the devil too much room in our lives. If that's the case, I can say for certain the devil would rather we be discouraged about our discouragement and give up completely on life than use it and the divine insights we derive from it as a springboard for future success and a productive second act of our lives and ministries. No matter what we've done, no matter what happened to us, no matter what we've been through, if we only get back up again, we can still be used by God, to the glory of God. It's time to get up and go strengthen our brothers and sisters. It's time to begin again.

PRACTICAL APPLICATION

A few weeks after picking myself up off the mat from the disappointment of not passing my DMin candidacy review on the first try, I had finally developed a game plan for a new, more focused, more relevant project. It was time to start recruiting participants for this updated project, and LinkedIn emerged as the social platform of choice for building my online community. Every recruit who participated earnestly was a blessing from God, but one person in particular truly touched my heart and had a profound impact on my rebuilding process. That was his goal all along.

Mike (as I'm calling him to protect his identity) is in his early-30s, as of this printing, is married, has two children, and is a very deep intellectual who is never short of thoughtful insights on any number of issues. He's actually one of the smartest people I've ever met, in cyberspace or in the flesh. I imagine he'll probably get a PhD one day. It's in him.

I see so much of myself in him, which I think is why we hit it off so well in the weeks leading up to the beginning of the project. When I visited some LinkedIn groups and began posting my appeal for participants, Mike was one of the first people to respond, and he did so enthusiastically. He was eager to participate in the project and was ready to share his story.

Recruiting participants took about a month, and it took a few weeks after that to get all of my requirements and logistics squared away so I could officially begin. In this time, Mike and I traded messages back and forth quite a bit and developed a good rapport that carried over into the project. He shared portions of his burnout story with me individually and with the group throughout the project. Through every discussion question, every opportunity for engagement, every activity, every week, Mike was my most consistent participant, always providing value to the conversation and, in the process, adding value to my life.

Mike's burnout experience happened not from the first chair as a Senior Pastor, but as a young, energetic, multi-talented Associate Pastor who buckled under the weight of being hit with too much responsibility at one time. His work began to affect his health, his marriage, and his psyche. He got burned out and became deeply depressed. His story is not unlike so many of us who have endured burnout.

The difference between Mike and so many others, though, is that, by the grace of God, he was able to make it back, fully recovering from burnout and ready to engage in full-time ministry again, once the right opportunity presented itself. Mike was blessed to be a part of a denomination that has a formal program for leading burnt-out pastors and their spouses through a process of recovery, renewal, and recommitment. He touts the program as instrumental in his ability to recover and position himself to do what so many are unable to do—return to a place of vitality and productivity in ministry after burning out.

This recovery program encouraged Mike so deeply and prepared him so well to re-enter ministry and re-engage that he was able to be a great encouragement to me throughout my project. When the project began, I was only six months removed from my previous church, so I was, without a doubt, still in the valley. Mike's insight, thoughtfulness, and consistent participation truly blessed me and empowered me to produced the best possible version of the project.

During our exit interview over the phone, Mike let me know just how intentional he was about his participation in my project. He saw the value of my study to the body of Christ and appreciated what I was trying to do. He resonated with it and told me very plainly that his primary motivation for participating and for being so consistent was to directly minister to me. I was absolutely floored by that and had no idea what to say, except to simply thank him from the bottom of my heart for his generosity and for all he had done to help me. I wouldn't be a Doctor of Ministry today without Mike.

At the time of that conversation, Mike was preparing for his third and final interview with a church to become its Lead Pastor. Praise be to God, he has since been hired by that church and has transitioned nicely into providing strong leadership for that congregation.

When searching for stories of people who have experienced some measure of recovery from the pain and shame of burnout in pastoral ministry, Mike's name should come up first. His is the success story of all success stories, and is a shining example of the point I've been trying to drive home throughout this book—there is life after pastoral burnout. I pray that one day, he will be compelled to share his story on a grander scale because if he blessed me as greatly as he did, I'm sure it will do the same for so many others.

Not everyone can be like Mike

Mike was blessed to be a part of a denomination that takes very seriously its mandate to not just train pastors for ministry and deploy them to churches, but to support and restore them when times get hard to a place of usefulness and productivity in the kingdom. Obviously, every pastor is not a part of Mike's denomination, unfortunately, and therefore does not have access to the type of training and therapy necessary to seek healing and restoration, not just of his or her ministry, but, more importantly, of his or her life in general.

It is because of this lack of access that I'm working as hard as I can to share this message of rebuilding life after burnout with the world. I want to work with denominations and independent religious organizations all over the world to help broken, burnt-out pastors find healing and restoration so they can return to living productive lives, whatever that might look like moving forward.

Furthermore, the anointing and desire to pastor in the local church may pass after the experience of burnout, not because someone becomes too weak to lead people post-burnout, but because that drive and sincerity to do so just might not be there anymore. I certainly don't have any desire to be a pastor anymore. My brief pastoral career was a very rewarding one, but I believe that ship has sailed for me. In enduring my burnout experience, I came to realize and fully embrace the fact that, while I took very seriously the office and responsibilities of a pastor, the position is outside of my sphere of genius. Being a pastor is nowhere near the best use of the gifts God has given me.

As I stated previously, I think Mike and I are very similar in a lot of ways, but our experiences and our callings are vastly different. My story doesn't look anything like his, nor does your story look like either of ours, and that's a good thing. Each of us was fearfully and wonderfully made by God to fulfill a specific kingdom purpose while we're on this side of eternity, so what works for one is just not going to work for all.

And I think that's what's most difficult about writing material on pastoral burnout. Negative statistics, statements of the problem, and lists of pitfalls concerning burnout are ubiquitous, while solutions aren't quite as readily available. Dr. Terry Wardle, Professor of Practical Theology and Director of the Institute of Formational Counseling at Ashland Theological Seminary, where I earned my MDiv, has been writing and teaching on personal spiritual renewal for decades and leads a fantastic workshop dealing with overcoming burnout in ministry, called "Why Leaders Lose Heart" [1].

Pastor Rick Warren has written and taught at various times on ministry burnout and has some valuable things to say about the subject [2]. Also, blogger and pastor Carey Nieuwhof has written, in my opinion, from all I've researched, the best individual article on steps leading to recovery from burnout in pastoral ministry [3].

Besides these materials, there still remains much to be researched and developed specifically on burnout recovery. No singular solution is going to work for everyone because such a blue pill does not exist. Such is why this final step in the rebuilding process is so important.

It's time to begin again

What step am I talking about? I'm talking about the step of re-engagement. After experiencing the hurt, the pain, the shame, the embarrassment of pastoral burnout, after you've gone back to your foundation to remember who and what are important in your life, after you've revisited the rudiments of the faith and the fundamentals of Christian living, after you've begun the work of putting your life back together again, it's time to re-engage with the community. It's time to begin again.

If you don't begin again, you rob yourself of the opportunity to bless someone else's life through what you've endured, and worse yet, you rob someone who needs the ministry God has placed in you. Burnout doesn't invalidate your ministry; it empowers you to do even greater ministry than you could have ever imagined.

Had Mike not begun again after going through his rebuilding process, I would have never him, he would have never sowed into my life, and you might not be reading this today. No matter how long it takes, at some point, you must re-engage.

Beginning again is going to look a little bit different for everyone. For my brother Mike, re-engagement for him meant faithfully working a secular job and strengthening his marriage and family relationships for a couple years until he recovered and was prepared to accept a Lead Pastor position.

For you, re-engagement may mean healing your mind, body, and spirit to the point where you feel comfortable attending corporate worship again. What might have happened to you might have been so catastrophic that it had the potential to make you question or even completely turn from your faith altogether, but you didn't, and that's miraculous in itself. You may never go back to vocational ministry, but you still have the opportunity to render tremendous service for God.

For me, re-engagement has meant studying burnout and building online community around it, completing my DMin on the subject, beginning to share my story over and over again to whomever would listen, and building a new ministry for myself wherein I can engage the community on the subject of burnout. I still preach here and there, but not too often. My wife and I also assist her mother's ministry. We have also found a great church that we visit regularly, but we're not anchored there or any other central location right now as official members.

It's not ideal, but it's where we are right now until further notice. I honestly don't know if I could deal with more local church responsibility than what I already have.

I have not gone into a cave (although it would have been really easy to do so at times), I have not lost my faith, I have not lost my will and desire to preach the gospel, and I am more encouraged now than ever about the direction of my life and ministry. Everything is not perfect, but I'm getting there; I'm doing the best I can. I'm doing the work. I'm beginning again. I'm rebuilding.

DEVOTIONAL POINTS

Reflect

1. Begin to connect the concepts we've discussed throughout the book. How do you stop blaming or shaming yourself? What must you do in this season to refocus on your family and, if necessary, reconnect and reconcile with them? What kind of community can you connect with to strengthen and encourage you? What non-ministry-related activities can you engage in to bring balance to your life? Can your faithfulness toward spiritual disciplines increase? Looking back on what you've been through, what would you do differently, given the new perspective you now have? How can you take greater ownership of your burnout experience to position yourself for more powerful ministry to others? How are you shaping or reshaping your story for greater impact? How are you reinventing yourself for this next season in your life?

2. Think about the absolute worst thing you did and/or that happened to you as a pastor. How has the memory of those moments burdened you during this season? Do you know or have you heard of anyone going through the same issues that contributed to your burnout? Have you gained some strength or insight as you've reflected on those

moments that you can use to help that person or anyone else in a similar situation? Consider all the people, even fellow pastors, whose lives could be forever changed by your getting back up, embracing your experiences and the stories they've produced, and reengaging the community, rather than bottling up your stories and hiding from the community.

3. Ask yourself and really consider what "beginning again" looks like to you personally. I want to emphasize here the word "what" rather than "where". As I've stated previously, I can't truly define burnout recovery for you because each of our experiences and callings are different. Recovery for me might mean traveling, speaking, writing, teaching in seminary, and having a successful church communications consultancy while serving as a staff pastor not in the first chair. Recovery for you may be finding gainful employment and working up the nerve to even step back in the local church again just for worship. It could mean taking a breather and working toward starting your own ministry. The most important thing to think on here is what you'll be doing in life and ministry, not where you'll be doing it. Don't judge your recovery based on someone else's timeline or location, for God's plans are for you and you only.

Read

1. Luke 22-24.
2. Blog post, "How I Recovered from Burnout: 12 Keys to Getting Back," by Carey Nieuwhof. I touched on this piece earlier, but it's worth mentioning again. This article, a followup to the aforementioned "9 Signs You're Burning Out in Leadership" post, is as thorough as a single blog post on burnout can be, as Nieuwhof writes eloquently and candidly on the experience of burnout, what he did and how long it took to recover, and what recovery or, as he termed it, "getting back" looked like for him. It's a very good perspective to read at this point in the rebuilding process.

Pray

#PrayForYourPastor

Pray that your pastor never gets to the point where he or she needs to "begin again" in this way. Hold your pastor's feet to the fire, keep him or her accountable, and don't become a yes man or woman for your pastor, but commit yourself to being the kind of church member who's easy to pastor. When you have a problem with your pastor, schedule an appointment and discuss it with him or her in private, rather than gossiping about it with people who are powerless to address it. If you're hospitalized but you're not dying, don't be extra critical of your pastor if he or she either doesn't make it to your bedside right away, or needs to send an associate pastor or elder to check on you. Don't call your pastor after 8:00pm unless it's an emergency.

Pray for the health and wellbeing of his or her spouse and children every chance you get. Go to your pastor with ideas you have about the ministry so he or she knows you're invested. Not only that, go with a proposal in hand and with a willingness in your heart to execute on those plans. Give generously and consistently. Whatever you think is a reasonable amount of yearly vacation time for your pastor, add a couple weeks to it.

And finally, pray you and your fellow members can resist approaching your pastor with anything other than a "Hello, how are you?" before worship begins. If you absolutely need to see your pastor before service, let it be because you're just dying to say you're praying for the Holy Spirit to move on his or her heart to preach the word with great boldness and power. Become, as Dr. Thom Rainer calls it in one of his podcast episodes, a PIPP—a *Pastoral Intercessory Prayer Partner* [4]. In short, pray you can be the kind of member who is a joy for any man or woman of God to pastor because if you do that, your pastor will less likely find him/herself in a burnout situation.

My prayer for you...

Father, in Jesus' name, I speak life over your recovering

servants. I know the best is yet to come in their lives. As I am encouraged about them, may they be even more encouraged at this point about their own future. God, speak to your people like never before. They need to hear your voice, and they need your direction as they discern the next steps in their lives and ministries. Will you have them to go back to pastoral ministry? Will you have them to sit in the first chair again? Or will you continue your ministry in them in a different way, in a different venue moving forward? Whatever you decide to do in them, however you move in them, make it clear, in the name of Jesus, so they know beyond a shadow of a doubt.

Help your people to pick themselves up, dust themselves off, take ownership of their story, and begin again, for there is still a great work to do, and there are too many souls that yet need to be saved for your rebuilding servants to sit on their gifts, downtrodden and emotional about their past. Strengthen your people, encourage them, build them back up, and make them living, breathing, walking testimonies of your saving grace and your healing power. May their latter be greater than their past, and may hungry souls all over the world be the beneficiaries thereof. I ask all these things in faith, in Jesus' name, Amen.

NOTES

INTRODUCTION
[1] Michael Hyatt, http://michaelhyatt.com.

1
[1] Carey Nieuwhof, "9 Signs You're Burning Out in Leadership," http://careynieuwhof.com/2013/07/9-signs-youre-burning-out-in-leadership/.

3
[1] Michael Hyatt, "5 Reasons You're Not Getting Traction with Your Platform," http://michaelhyatt.com/traction.html.

[2] Shaun King, "Stressed Out Pastors, Crazy Sins, and the Death of Pastor Zach Tims," http://www.shauninthecity.com/2011/08/stressed-out-pastors-crazy-sins-and-the-death-of-pastor-zach-tims.html.

4
[1] Cliff Ravenscraft, Podcast Answerman [podcast], http://podcastanswerman.com.

[2] Jackie Bledsoe, Jr. "How to Be an Ephesians 5 Husband for Your Proverbs 31 Wife," http://blackandmarriedwithkids.com/2013/12/how-to-be-an-ephesians-5-husband-for-your-proverbs-31-wife/.

5

[1] Authentic Christian Community, http://community.cylarconsulting.com. This is the website I built and used primarily for my DMin project. Much of the content is still protected, but enough of the site is public to read and find out more about the project.

6

[1] A Coney Island is a type of Greek American restaurant very popular in the state of Michigan. For more info, visit the Coney Island on Wikipedia: http://en.wikipedia.org/wiki/Coney_Island_(restaurant).

7

[1] Bo Lane, *Why Pastors Quit*, pp. 22-24.

[2] Thom Rainer, "Ten Joy Stealers in Ministry (And How to Get It Back)," http://thomrainer.com/2015/02/25/ten-joy-stealers-ministry-get-back/.

8

[1] Dale Wolery, "Where There Is Smoke…" http://www.clergyrecovery.com/?page_id=615.

11

[1] Jeff Goins, *The Portfolio Life* [podcast], https://itunes.apple.com/us/podcast/id844091351.

[2] Mihaly Csikszentmihalyi, "Flow, the secret to happiness [speech]," http://www.ted.com/talks/mihaly_csikszentmihalyi_on_flow?language=en.

[3] Eric Thomas, "Levels [speech excerpt]," Greatness is Upon You Mixtape, https://www.youtube.com/watch?v=fhJ1PrmZlMg.

[4] "Mixtape (definition)," http://www.urbandictionary.com/define.php?term=mixtape.

Usually produced by recording artists, Dr. Eric Thomas is the first motivational speaker to ever produce a mixtape of his own. At the time of this printing, he has three such recordings, featuring excerpts from over 20 years of speaking, set to music mostly of the hip-hop/rap genre.

12

[1] Terry Wardle, "Why Leaders Lose Heart // Ashland Theological Seminary [video clip]," https://www.youtube.com/watch?v=rmo6unnJ-xs.

[2] Rick Warren, "Four Steps to Reversing Ministry Burnout," http://pastors.com/burnout-recovery/.

[3] Carey Nieuwhof, "How I Recovered From Burnout: 12 Keys to Getting Back," http://careynieuwhof.com/2013/07/how-i-recovered-from-burn-out-12-keys-to-getting-back/.

[4] Thom Rainer, "Nine Keys to Successful Sermon Preparation – Rainer on Leadership #097 [podcast episode]," http://thomrainer.com/2015/02/10/nine-keys-successful-sermon-preparation-rainer-leadership-097/.

Notes

ACKNOWLEDGMENTS

This is hard. So many of you have made such a difference in my life over the past few years, and I don't want to slight you in any way, but I can only call a few of you by name. As the cliché goes, please charge it to my head and not my heart.

Chariece, you are my queen, my best friend, and I love you so much. The sacrifices you've made to help me achieve my dreams have been unspeakable. I look forward to returning the favor. Thank you, baby. The half hasn't been told…

Candace and Jada, thank you for constantly reminding me what and who are really important. I love you.

Dad (Ken Cylar), you've never not been there for me. How many black men in America can say that? Thank you.

Dr. Urias Beverly and my DMin colleagues at Ecumenical Theological Seminary, you've seen me through some hard times professionally, but you've stayed patient with me, and I thank you.

Dr. Robert Seymour, thank you for challenging every jot and tittle of my dissertation. Your serious but friendly scrutiny made it infinitely better.

Dr. Charles Edward Clark, Jr., thank you for challenging me to pivot the focus of my research. I was resistant at first, but I realize now it was for my good; it's helped produce the work that's before you now and has shaped the course of the rest of my life forever.

Dr. Oscar King III, you weren't with me for the entire journey, but without even knowing it, you imparted a lot in me in such a short period of time. Thank you.

Bo Lane, your book and your site have been a blessing to me. I was at a different place personally and spiritually when I found this material, and you've greatly encouraged me and helped me tremendously to get to where I am today. Even more so, your genuine enthusiasm about and endorsement of this book from the very beginning have blessed me beyond measure. Thank you.

Bishop Jeronn C. Williams and Pastor General Dr. LaToya K. Williams, I've been gone from the church for an entire decade, but all I am today as a man of God is because of how you both poured into me during my formative years in ministry at New Life International Family Church. I still count you as my spiritual parents and am eternally grateful for all you've done for me. Thank you.

To my crew—Chris Preston, Robert Harmon, Jr., Aaron Harmon, and Donald Wine II—you guys' friendship and brotherhood were invaluable to me in childhood, and now, even more so in adulthood. I don't know what I'd do without you guys. Thank you.

Jesus, nothing I could say could possibly be sufficient, so I'll just say thank you.

ABOUT THE AUTHOR

A former pastor in the African Methodist Episcopal Church, **Dr. Marcus A. Cylar** is a professional editor, writer, and speaker. He recently completed his Doctor of Ministry studies at Ecumenical Theological Seminary in Detroit, with his dissertation entitled, "Building community through social media to tackle pastoral burnout". Marcus and his wife, Chariece, are the parents of two beautiful girls, Candace and Jada. They are also consultants helping churches, nonprofits, and small businesses organize and plan more efficiently, communicate more effectively, and use technology with greater savvy.

Eradicating pastoral burnout has become one of Marcus' chief passions in life, and he's working earnestly to write and speak on, as well as build community around, the recovery from and avoidance of pastoral burnout. He wants to hear from anyone who has a story about their experiences with burnout in pastoral ministry with or the effects thereof and appreciates input from all who share his passion for tackling this most dire issue in the body of Christ.

Dr. Cylar can be reached on Twitter **@pastorcylar** or by email at **me@marcusacylar.com**.

www.ingramcontent.com/pod-product-compliance
Lightning Source LLC
LaVergne TN
LVHW041251080426
835510LV00009B/691